How I Grieve

Praying for Sunshine, Strength, and Peace

B. Taylor Mason

Nancy,

I sure do miss our days at UA. Those were great times! It's my pleasure to know you.

Love,

B. Taylor Mason

ISBN-13: 978-1499235029

ISBN-10: 149923502X

Also Available as ebooks from B. Taylor Mason

How I Grieve Series

I Grieve: Praying for Sunshine

I Still Grieve: Praying for Strength

Forever I Grieve: Praying for Peace

For my mother, Marie, and my sister, Kim, who joined me in Dad's journey from diagnosis to death.

I love you both more than you know.

For Brennan, Brandt, Ellie, and Riley--Pop loved you with his whole heart.

For Jeff, my love, always.

For Brennan and Brandt—You were both the best things I have ever done. I love you with my whole life.

For the 7th grade class of 2014 at GMS. Thanks for putting up with my mood swings. (No ignorance)

To my dad, Riley, who will forever be in my heart.

To our Pop who set the bar high for grandfathers everywhere.

You were our "King of the World" (Point of Grace)

"I'll See You Again" (Westlife)

To Mikee—thanks for the memories.

How I Grieve

Praying for Sunshine, Strength, and Peace

Book One

I Grieve: Praying for Sunshine

From diagnosis to death, this book follows an adult daughter's journey with her ill father. In just under a year, a vibrant man succumbs to an aggressive form of lymphoma. He leaves behind a family who struggles to adapt to the loss and provide a legacy to honor his memory. This story is an honest account of the daughter's raw emotion and her attempt to accept the loss of her father and continue living.

Table of Contents

Chapter 1—I Grieve

Chapter 2—The Third Time Is Not a Charm

Chapter 3—He's a Fighter

Chapter 4—Summertime Second Opinion

Chapter 5—Sweet Home Alabama

Chapter 6—Casseroles and Anger Management

Chapter 7—Can He Hear Me Now?

Chapter 8—Legacy of his Love

Chapter 9—The Struggle

Chapter 10—Necessary Evil

Chapter 11—Praying for Sunshine

I Grieve

Waiting to die. The phrase makes me a bit queasy. I realize that we are all, from the moment we are born, waiting to die. Some of us will die suddenly. Some of us will die from accidents, disease, or sickness. Some of us will be victims of violent crime. Some of us will die as children, reckless teenagers, or old age. I never figured I would be sitting with my father waiting for him to die. I had always assumed he and my mom would live into old age, as their parents both lived well into their eighties. I thought they would both be around forever— or at least until they were admitted into a nursing home and died a peaceful death in their sleep. I did not imagine holding my father's hand and watching to see if he would take another breath. That was the longest summer of my life.

I am 43 years old and have recently buried my father. How blessed I was to have him around for 43 years. How sad and broken I am now that he is gone. How will I continue? How will my sister, mother, children, and nieces continue? It is not going to be easy.

I grieve. They grieve. I have heard that grieving is cleansing for the soul. So far, I have not found that to be true. Time heals all wounds. Sure it does. Right now, I cannot believe all the clichés. I miss my daddy. End of story.

The beginning of my father's story starts here. My father was a giant among men. He was a son, brother, husband, teacher, coach, farmer, father, and friend. He was not perfect, but lived his life as an example of the true strength of a man. He had strong convictions about right and wrong, and expected those around him to uphold those same convictions. He strove to be fair, in all things. He had a competitive nature, rivaled only by his love for his family. Nothing made him happier than watching his girls and grandchildren participate in sports. We knew he loved us and was proud of us. He told us these things, but also showed us by his actions. He taught us to shoot guns, bait a hook, change flat tires, and scared our boyfriends. He yelled at officials of sporting events when he felt we were done wrong. He wore a Cheer Dad shirt when my sister competed in cheer competitions. He was our defender, on and off the court and field. Even when we failed him, he still loved us, just as a father should do.

The Third Time is Not a Charm

Daddy died after a fight against a third form of cancer. He had previously defeated prostate cancer and Hodgkin's Lymphoma. The third cancer, T Cell lymphoma, killed him. There is no other way to say it. The cancer invaded his body, filling his organs, replacing open spaces with masses, slowly working its way through his entire body, cutting off all his body's attempts to live. I watched this cancer consume his body. His lymph nodes swelled to form hardened lumps, which caused him some pain and irritation. He rarely complained, even when his treatment included multiple bone marrow biopsies, chemotherapy, and various blood tests and scans. He suffered in silence, until his pain caused him to moan in his sleep. Toward the end, nothing could take his pain away. He refused help getting up and around until he had no other choice. He was a man's man, insisting that he could do everything himself, insisting that he could beat this cancer, insisting that he would do everything he could to live. He did all he could, but in the end, there was nothing he or anyone else could do to conquer cancer.

His journey with this killing cancer started with an unusual knot in a lymph node in his groin. A local surgeon removed it and sent it for testing. He had previously had the same surgery with results that indicated nothing more than a benign mass—no cancer, no trouble, just a small incision and instructions to watch the area carefully. More than a year later, the second lump appeared. Our family tried to brush off the proposed lymphoma diagnosis from the surgeon. I remember him saying, "I was almost certain it was lymphoma last time and I was wrong. I think it is lymphoma this time. We will just have to wait and see what the test results show." The surgeon did not appear to be alarmed and we, mostly, took his words to heart. This second surgery and lump appeared to be the same as the first. How wrong our assumptions were.

I will never forget the call from my mom. It was a steamy Friday night in September 2012. Being from the South, football, played by any age group, is king. My son and I were going to watch our local high school team at an away football game. My sister had arrived earlier. My mom called while I was making the 30-minute drive. She told me that she had heard from the doctor on that Friday afternoon and my dad did test positive for lymphoma. I asked if she had called my sister. "Yes," Mom replied, "and she will need to lean on you, just like I will." My breath caught in my throat. How could this be? The lump was supposed to be nothing. Now, it turns out, cancer had invaded our family in a harsh way. There was no way to avoid it any longer. I continued to the game and my sister and I looked at each other in shock. I knew she had been crying, but she had responsibilities to attend before we could sit and discuss this. That was absolutely the longest game of my life. Those four quarters were endless. I was anxious and apprehensive, uncertain about exactly what we would do next. The game seemed trivial. Losing the game was only a minor inconvenience compared with gearing up to fight a cancer battle, where losing would mean death.

He's a Fighter

The fight led to our next step...finding an oncologist. We turned to our nearest teaching hospital, UAB (University of Alabama at Birmingham). They provided fine care, but ultimately, the cancer would be too much. Things started with a general meeting with the doctor. Tests were done and done again. A bone marrow biopsy was scheduled. CT scans and PET scans consumed Dad's life. My mom, my sister, and I were there through it all. We met with the doctors, waited during the tests, the chest port surgery, the chemotherapy visits. We made countless trips to Birmingham during the six months of treatment. We stayed with them, spending long days and some nights at the hospital and a friend's home. Every few weeks revealed a new problem. At some points, Dad's blood counts were too low for treatment. He caught the flu and had pneumonia. These additional illnesses required hospitalization and we all took turns staying with him. We all had to take infectious precautions, which meant masks, gloves, and lots of hand sanitizer.

After about six months, he had a period of around six weeks without any type of treatment, waiting for another scheduled PET scan to decide if more treatment was required. During this time, he and my mom took a trip with two friends to Europe. This trip was their 50th anniversary trip, celebrated with friends from college, including the pastor who married them, Robert and his wife Florence. It was an extensive trip including airplanes, trains, and taxis. Luggage was light and many visits were on the itinerary. My father returned from this trip exhausted. While he was glad it made my mom happy, physically, he was tired. We soon found out why he was so tired. His PET scan revealed some cancer still in his body. The biopsy from a lymph node in his neck now showed a different type of cancer, T Cell Lymphoma.

Summertime Second Opinion

At this point, we decided to seek a second opinion. While we were pleased with UAB and the staff there, the hospital has a reputation as a heart/transplant center, not a premiere cancer center. We scheduled a visit at M.D. Anderson Cancer Center in Houston, Texas. His first appointment was in early June. As teachers, my sister and I were out of school for the summer and could help with arrangements. We researched places to stay near the hospital. We helped get test results and samples sent to MDA. We figured flight and car rental costs. Finally, my mom decided to drive the 13-hour trip to Houston so she would have her own vehicle and save some money. A distant relative offered them a guest room in her home. With an appointment scheduled for a Monday, we packed up the cars and headed to Houston early on Saturday. I drove the lead vehicle and my mom drove her car, following me through Alabama, Mississippi, and Louisiana. We stopped for the night about three hours away from Houston. Everyone was exhausted. My father was feeling poorly and needed some food. Turns out, he also was suffering from pneumonia, but we did not know that at the time. After supper, we checked into a nearby Hampton Inn. Dad still felt ill and spiked a fever. He began vomiting and was unsteady on his feet. We got him to the restroom and I made a middle-of-the-night trip to Wal-Mart for ibuprofen. It was a long night. No one got much sleep. I am just thankful I was able to make the trip with my folks. The situation was not one I would have wanted my mom to face alone.

The next morning we drove on into Houston and found Cousin Peggy's home. She was a Godsend to our family during this time. She had prepared a delicious lunch for us and welcomed us into her home as if we had known her all our lives. The fact that we had never met meant nothing to her. We got my mom and dad settled in for naps and I called my sister to give her an update. She was not able to begin this part of the journey with us, for she has two small children. My children were older and more able to take care of themselves. Strangely, her phone kept going straight to voicemail. Not much later, I received a Facebook notification from her with a photo of her loading a plane to Houston. She instructed me to be at the airport that evening to pick her up. Like any good sister, I followed her orders. Unfamiliar with Houston, I took Peggy with me to guide me through the traffic. Thankfully, Sunday evenings are nothing like rush hour around Houston. We made it to the airport with time to spare and picked up my sister with no trouble. My folks were so glad to see her. Our family was complete again as we faced the cancer monster head on the next morning.

After a restless night, we arrived early to MDA for my dad's scheduled appointment. Various paperwork had to be completed, as well as documents scanned and insurance applied. We finally were called back to an exam room. My father rested quietly on the bed. My mom, sister, and I worried about his condition. The oncologist entered the room and introduced himself. After a physical examination, he felt that my father needed to be admitted to the hospital for observation and treatment for pneumonia and possibly a fungal infection.

The cancer treatment would have to wait. The first priority was getting him well from the current ailment. Two weeks of antibiotics, antifungal medicines, biopsies from lymph nodes and bone marrow, followed by 3 days of intensive IV administered home health antibiotics and he was pronounced well enough to return to Alabama and begin cancer treatment. The second opinion was the same as the first opinion. Additional chemotherapy, on a different schedule, would begin almost immediately. Upon this announcement, we said our goodbyes to Cousin Peggy and began the long trip home. The trip home was surprisingly uneventful.

Sweet Home Alabama

After returning to Alabama, Dad headed back to UAB to begin treatment again. This chemo was administered on a different schedule. Instead of every three weeks, this treatment was to be given weekly. He suffered through a couple of treatments then started having spells of fever, uncontrollable shaking (almost like a seizure), and unresponsiveness. He was not unconscious, but was in a daze, separated from reality, and unsure about what transpired during that time. After he came out of the spell, he was back to his regular self. One of these spells happened while we were waiting to visit the doctor before his next chemotherapy infusion. We placed him in a wheelchair and took him to a room right off the lobby. The nurses came in to help, but there was nothing to be done, except let the spell continue. Obviously, the chemo was not working and the decision was made, with the doctor, to suspend further treatment. We were taking Dad home with hospice. No other options were available to treat him. His age and previous health problems prevented any different treatment. We were basically waiting for my dad to die.

Hospice workers were waiting for us when we returned to their house. They brought a hospital bed, medicines for pain and sleep, and an assortment of other medical equipment that we hoped we would never have to use. When the nurse first met us and assessed my father, she was not optimistic about his condition. She encouraged us to spend as much time with him as possible before the inevitable happened. As I watched him that night, I was afraid that might be the last night we had with him. The grandchildren came in to hug and kiss him, just in case things headed south quickly. My mom, sister, and I took turns sitting by his bedside that night. In the morning, he felt better. Our spirits lifted. I know it was false hope, but somehow, my father had found some strength and was not ready to go just yet. In the back of my mind, I continued to remember that we were still in a waiting game.

Casseroles and Anger Management

Throughout the summer of 2013, my family and my sister's family spent as much time with my dad as possible. One or both of us stayed at their home every night. We did not want to be away, as the uncertainty of what might happen was too great. We also did not want to leave all the nightly care to my mom. Now, let me say this: my mom is one of the strongest women I know. She has endured all my father's health issues, including the times he was not expected to live, with grace and an undying love for my dad. She has been beside him through the good times and the bad times. She was his rock. She kept great notes about all his medical conditions and provided excellent care for him during trying times. While I did not doubt her ability to help him, I did not feel it was fair to her to be the only one there during the night. I wanted to be available in case she needed help. My father was 6'2'' and about 200 pounds. My mom is closer to 5'7'' and 130 pounds. The size difference mattered.

We have absolutely the best friends, family, coworkers, and neighbors. All these people treated my family like royalty during my father's illness and death. So many different people brought dinners and lunches. We always had something to offer any guests. As my father was a coach and teach before his retirement, he had visits and phone calls from players, managers, colleagues, friends, and distant family. He had such a wonderful time reliving ballgames and tournament times with former players. He prayed with his church friends. He talked about school with colleagues. He talked farming with friends. My dad thoroughly enjoyed all the visitors he had during his illness. He visited with the grandchildren and watched them play in the yard. He supervised his grandson cutting the grass.

Most people have the best of intentions when they ask, "How are you? How is your sister? How is your mom doing?" I answer with the standard response, "We are ok. We are all fine. It is different, but we are getting used to it." What I really find myself feeling inside is this: I was not dwelling on the loss until you brought it up by asking me how we are all coping with the loss. I was doing fine. Now I am thinking about my dad and how much I miss him. I am replaying in my head the highlights of our time together. I am trying to remember the last year of his life, where he fought his third bout with cancer. I am taken back to their bedroom, where he took his last breath. I hate it. I hate every thought of it. I want him here, not dead and buried. I will not tell you this. I will lie and say, "We're doing okay."

Now I am mad at me and mad at you. I am mad at me because I cannot lock all the memories away for a time when I am more prepared to deal with them. I am mad because I am too emotionally unstable to know how to adequately respond when this barrage of memories assaults me. I am mad because my dad is gone and now my mom is alone. I am mad because this means more responsibility for me, just in making sure she is ok. I am the older daughter, so I am the one she turns to and leans on now. My children are older and I am more available to help her. I am mad because I was not ready for him to go.

I never worried about Mom when Dad was alive; they took care of each other and called if my sister or I were needed. The worry I had for my father during his illness has simply transferred to my mom. She is now alone and I worry that she may be sick or hurt and unable to call me. I worry that she is depressed. I know she cries, but she doesn't want us to know. I am angry because she is alone.

I am mad at you because you brought it up. I know you were trying to be kind, offering prayers, or a helping hand. Wanting to know if there was anything we needed. Well, what we all need is our father back. Not like he was, sick and cancerous, hurting yet stoic, but like he was before his illness. The times when he played with the grandchildren, took them for rides in his truck, and bought them Coke and M&M's to spoil their supper. The times when he went to the volleyball matches, peewee football games, dance recitals, and school plays; gave them spending money; and always bought whatever wrapping paper or seat cushion they were selling for school. I want him back sitting in the den watching

Alabama football and talking about the SEC. I am mad at you because you made me remember how things were, and realize, once again, that those things will never be again.

I am mad at myself because I never know how I will react when I think about him. I am mad that I can hear a song on the radio and it brings me to tears. I am mad that he will not be here for the things I consider important: Halloween, Thanksgiving, Christmas, Valentine's Day, his birthday, and Sunday lunches after church. I am mad that he will not be around for my mom, and the milestones in my life and my sister's life. He will miss many of the rites of passage of his grandchildren. Let us face it; I am stuck in the angry phase of grief. I have no idea when I will move on to acceptance, if ever.

Can He Hear Me Now?

I visit his grave often, more often than I ever imagined I would. I think about his body stuck in that coffin. I wonder what happens to his clothes, his belt, his handkerchief, his tie tack, and his knife. He was buried with all these things, because in life, he would never have been caught without a handkerchief or a pocketknife. How could we bury him without those? We buried him in a fancy suit, dress shirt, and tie, all of his favorites. I sit on a tombstone, not his, that is near his grave. He was buried under a tree in a lovely section of the cemetery. I can drive my vehicle right up to the edge of his plot. The grass is still just sod. It hasn't grown together with the remainder of the lawn. There are still rocky patches from the crew digging his grave. I want to pick up all the rocks and throw them as far as I can. It would be a great stress reliever. However, instead, I just clear them from the top of his grave area. I cry as I stand beside his grave. Tears somehow leak out, no matter how hard I try to stop them. I tell him how hard it is to continue going through the motions without him here. I tell him about my family, my mom, my sister, her girls, and all the struggles we have. We placed flowers on his grave at Christmas, and visited again on his birthday in January. Individually we each visit other times as well. We three have yet to visit his grave and leave without tears. His grave is across from a veteran's memorial area with flags. I have chosen the blue one as a representative of him. If the blue flag waves in the breeze, I believe it means he hears me. How sad is that?

My father was what a country song would call a "tractor man." He loved farm equipment and had three tractors: a red Massey Ferguson, a blue Ford, and a green John Deere. The John Deere received damage in early 2011 in a tornado that destroyed much of his farmland and demolished a barn. The Massey Ferguson and Ford tractors are now at his horse farm near my home. I can ride by and see them sitting under the awning of the brand new red barn he built for his horses. He was so proud of the land and those horses. I can still picture him riding the tractor around bush hogging the land to clear all the brush and weeds. To this day, whenever I see a tractor, I feel like my dad is present with me. The day of his funeral, as we were riding to the graveside service, we had to wait for a tractor to cross the road before we could continue. I often see tractors in unlikely places. On the way to watch a football game, I saw three different tractors parked in front yards. This was odd. I knew that was his way of reassuring me that he is well and wonderful in heaven.

As I write this, I am flooded with memories of time with him. I recall driving his red tractor when I was just a kid, maybe around age seven. I remember going to his farm, sitting at auctions, riding a small motorcycle, riding horses, pitching softball, shooting basketball, shooting guns, driving his truck before I had a license. These are just a few of the things I miss about him. Even though I am older now, some things are just better with Daddy.

Watching the slide show at Dad's funeral brought back so many memories. Sometimes I watch it now just to remember. There were pictures from his entire life: pictures with my grandparents and his sisters, newlywed photos with Mom, pictures of me and my sister when we were born, snapshots of him holding each of his three granddaughters and one grandson, pictures where he was the father of the bride, twice, pictures of his oldest granddaughter's proms, pictures of him riding a go-kart with his grandson, pictures of his two younger granddaughters' birthdays and recitals, and pictures of him with Mom on cruises, vacations, and a 50th anniversary trip to Switzerland, Paris, and Germany, only months before his death. These photos are bittersweet. They bring back the precious memories of times spent with him, but at the same time, they serve to make me miss him more. I know that there will be no more times with him like this. There will be times of sadness and despair, laced with joy from memories. These reminders make me miss him even more.

Legacy of His Love

He usually had kind words for all around him. I remember him telling my daughter Brennan, his oldest granddaughter, that she was his favorite. He told my son, Brandt, that he was so proud of the responsibilities he was taking with helping Mom and was so pleased to see his progress in football and making all A's in school. He told my older niece, Ellie, that she had the kindest soul and the most beautiful freckles and red hair. He told my sister that her baby girl, named Riley for my dad, "was perfect." I remember these things about my dad. He never failed to tell my sister and me that he was proud of us and he loved us. His last spoken words were telling my mom he loved her. Sometimes remembering these things keeps the pain at bay for a while. The pain comes from knowing, but not realizing, how blessed we were when he was alive, and recognizing that many things are just not as good without him.

After my father's retirement, he purchased a small area of land and had a few horses there. The land is near my home and work. I often ride by and visit with the horses. They remind me of my dad. They are big and strong, yet gentle. During his illness, my sister and I, as well as a close family friend, took care of the horses. One of my father's favorite things to do when he felt well enough to get out was have my mom drive him to his farm and look at the horses. He would also ride to watch his only grandson practice junior high football. My father died the week before my son's first football game, so the fact that Pop could watch practice is reassuring to me. Not long after practice started, my Dad and my son had a "manly" talk. My father shared his thoughts about improving in football with my son, as well as things he thought all boys should be prepared for in life. He passed along some great advice to my son that day. I cherish these moments.

The Struggle

The last week of my father's life rocked me to my core. Somehow, we all knew things were drawing to a close. We had hired a sitter to stay at the home to help Mom with the house and Dad with anything and everything. Until that time, Dad had refused to receive any help from Big Ed. My sister and I started a new school year, and I stayed at their house at night, returning to my own home before sunrise. We went to school for about a week before the dramatic deterioration. I was at school and received a call from my mom. Dad was not himself. He insisted on doing things his way, but was physically unable to do so. He was angry at the situation, at Mom, at Big Ed. I rushed to their home and tried to talk to him. He seemed to be in the midst of a spell, so I just helped get him into bed and tried to comfort my mom. This was the beginning of the end.

My father spent the remaining time of his life medicated, resting in bed. The hospice nurses advised us that he would probably only live another 72 hours. My sister and I took off work and barely left the house. I took my son to school and later to football practice. I welcomed guests and family to visit. I worked on the obituary. My sister and Mom worked on pictures for the slide show at the wake. We made calls to extended family and friends. Arrangements for the preacher and musicians were completed. Everything was done that could be done. Again, we were just waiting for him to die.

On Tuesday, August 27, everyone was at Mom and Dad's house. My son had finished football practice and my family had all congregated at their house along with my sister's family. We ate supper and then the kids began their homework. We were sitting with Dad in his room and suddenly Mom said, "His breathing is funny." We rushed the kids out and let the husbands come in. My mom, sister, and I all held Dad's hands and told him how much we loved him. He fought so hard. While we watched, he struggled for breath. He kept fighting. We prayed for him to let go and pass on to heaven. We told him to go. We begged him to go. He was not going to go easily. He continued to draw a ragged breath every 30 seconds or so. The hospice nurse was with us and watched as he fought. I turned my mom's head away from watching him. I did not want her to see him struggle to live. Finally, he took his last breath and we all watched as the color faded from his face. As long as I live, I will never forget those last moments of his life— his struggle to stay with us. Those moments were the closest I have ever been to Heaven, but absolutely the hardest thing I have ever had to see.

The myriad of emotions that passed through me at that time is indescribable. I was overjoyed that my father was now healed, celebrating his life in heaven, shooting hoops with his friends and teammates who had passed on before him. At the same time, my heart was broken, mourning and longing for the father I would never have again; I wanted the summer to begin again so I would have more time with him. A different struggle started now, not for him, but for all of those who loved him and remained behind. Death is welcomed for the sickened person, but dreaded for those who are left to mourn.

Necessary Evil

The coroner and funeral home staff came to the house and took my daddy's body away. We were left there without him. We chose his clothes for the funeral. We called his sister, nieces and nephew. Mom called his best friends and asked them to be pallbearers. Mom's best friend came over to console her. My sister and I updated everyone via Facebook. We were all functioning in a state of shock. While his death was expected, it was much more violent than I had imagined it would be. The thing we had both dreaded for our sake, and desired for his sake, had happened. His pain was gone; ours was just beginning.

The time between his death on Tuesday night and his wake on Thursday night passed in a blur. One of the most difficult tasks to complete was meeting with the funeral home staff. The funeral was prepaid but many decisions remained. An allowance was provided for flowers, the obituary, and copies of the death certificate. We chose a fabulous black and silver casket with beautiful red and white roses. The obituary was lengthy but worth every cent it cost. It described the legacy this man left to all. Last, we looked at plots and chose the best one for him. That day was long and tiring, and I completely hated all that we had to do. It was one of the worst parts of the entire funeral.

My father's wake was scheduled from five to seven P.M. on Thursday night. My family arrived there at around three P.M. We met the funeral home staff and viewed my father for the first time since his death. I hate to sound clichéd, but he did look quite good, considering he was dead. His eyes were closed and his coloring was just right. He was wearing the handsome suit and had on his watch and glasses. I could not help myself. I touched his head. His skin was cool, not cold, as I had imagined it would be. I wanted to cover him with a blanket. We steeled ourselves for the onslaught of visitors who would stream through the church doors at five that evening. We watched the slideshow and cried. No one tells you how horrific that evening is and how long it lasts.

The next morning was the funeral. It was terrible. We had the service at our local Baptist church, where we are members. We arrived around nine and spent time in prayer and visiting with many friends who were unable to attend the wake. My sister, my children, my nieces, and I wrote notes to Dad and placed them into the casket to be buried with him.   The most difficult moment was saying the last goodbye before the funeral staff closed his casket. That image will be forever etched in my memory.

We all walked to the back of the church and waited for the signal to head back up the aisle. We sat in the front pew of the church. The casket was straight in front of me. To each side of the casket were many mementos and photos of my father and our family. I saw his cowboy hats, his belt buckles, his worn farm boots. There were pictures of him playing basketball, holding the grandchildren, and at both his wedding and at his farm. I saw his letterman jacket from Livingston, and his Flair Hair hat from his chemo treatments. I remember little of the actual service. My uncle sang and one of my father's past basketball players told some stories about him. Robert, the pastor who had married my mom and dad, also spoke his eulogy. How precious that my father was wed and buried by one of his closest friends. At the end of the service, we loaded into our cars and headed to the cemetery for the graveside portion of the funeral.

The graveside service was paralyzing. I guess that was the point where everything became real. The box that held my father was going into the ground and I would never see him or it again. I would only see the mound of sod-covered dirt that marked his final resting place. The horror of the moments before paled in comparison to that time. We sat under a tent, my sister and I holding our mother's hand, and listened to a short speech and prayer about how this box did not really hold my father. His soul was gone and only his body remained here to be buried. When the final prayer was said and we were expected to depart from the cemetery, we didn't want to leave. We picked flowers from the spray on top of his casket. We loitered, shooting daggers at the workers waiting nearby to lower the casket and replace the earth. Finally, we helped my mom into the car and, unable to look back, drove away to a life usurped by reality.

The women of the church prepared a repast, so we returned to dine with friends and family. After enjoying this meal and time together, my mom, sister, and I changed clothes and ventured back to the cemetery. In a span of three hours, so much had changed there. The tent and chairs were removed; the casket buried. Flowers marked the spot where sod covered the newly filled grave. Two large flower arrangements remained standing near the head of the grave. One was a mix of fall flowers; the other, a basketball themed arrangement provided by the grandchildren. My heart swelled with both sorrow and pride as I remembered my dad.

Praying for Sunshine

One thing that really makes me miss my father is the knowledge that my children and my nieces will miss seeing what a special man he was. My daughter and my son, ages 18 and 13 respectively, were more exposed to his kindness than my nieces, aged nine and three. The youngest will barely remember how much fun her Pop was. She will not have trips to the farm, riding in his lap on the 4-wheeler, fishing from the pier in his backyard. Those two will never get to drive his truck on the dirt roads at his farm, with him patiently explaining the rules of the road. They will never again get to sit in his lap and eat snacks and drink Coke. They will never know how much fun he was and how he loved to spoil his grandchildren. My children will not have him around for graduations, weddings, and births of their children. He is no longer around to celebrate accomplishments and suffer disappointments. There is no one who can take his place.

As a child, I often thought my father was larger than life. As an adult, I realized that most children have the same case of hero worship about their parents. Most adults do not remain mesmerized by the ability of one man to exemplify standards above those of the world. Most adults move past the stage of infatuation with a hero and lean toward the idea that each person has excellent qualities in his or her own right. This was not the case with my father. I had no idea that so many people held him in such high regard. In order to further the legacy of my father, my family decided to establish a scholarship to Gadsden State Community College for an aspiring high school athlete. The Riley Whitaker Memorial Scholarship will award a scholarship to its first recipient from the 2014 graduating class.

My family faces many challenges, still. The tombstone is ordered but has not been completed or installed. We have seen drawings of what to expect. The actual stone, I am sure, will bring tears, again. Important occasions will bring tears. Tomorrow I celebrate my 44th birthday. I will not celebrate it with my father, but I will have the rest of my family around. I feel certain that tomorrow will be a day with mixed emotions. My father always insisted on picking up the check when our entire family went out to eat. Tomorrow, that job will belong to my mother. While I am happy to celebrate another year in my life, it has been a difficult and tumultuous year. So many things are different, never to be the same again. The impact of one unexpected phone call in September 2012 is numbing. A single word, cancer, changed everything for my family.

Throughout this journey, my father kept his sense of humor. He laughed, joked, and flirted with the nurses. He would not let any of us see his hurt or pain. In the end, when he could laugh no more, he resigned himself to the inevitable. He had quotes for every occasion and this one seemed perfect to let us know that, while he would continue the fight, he knew the finish line was in sight. My father, a former Coach of the Year and Hall of Famer, told all of us, "You win some, you lose some, and some get rained out." Through this season of rain, I pray for peace; I pray for strength; I pray for sunshine.

Book Two

I Still Grieve: Praying for Strength

Six months after the death of her father from an aggressive form of lymphoma, an adult daughter attempts to reconcile her grief with the joy of her memories. The memories cause mixed emotions— emotions of love, pride, and loss. She explores the time after death, including all the rites of passage the family has survived without their father. Holidays, birthdays, and celebrations are all bittersweet, due to the grief that has taken root in her heart. Follow the family's emotions and actions, based on honoring the legacy of her father, through this second book in the How I Grieve series.

Table of Contents

Chapter 1 Missing Person

Chapter 2 Family Tradition

Chapter 3 "Above the Grass"

Chapter 4 One Million Dollars

Chapter 5 Flair Hair

Chapter 6 Guilt by Association

Chapter 7 Superhero

Chapter 8 Pocketknives and the DMV

Chapter 9 One Day at a Time

Chapter 10 Everything Changes

Chapter 11 Cabin Fever

Chapter 12 Snowpocalypse

Chapter 13 Home is Where the Heart Is

Chapter 14 "Where is Poppa?"

Chapter 15 Holiday Heartache

Chapter 16 Cemetery Celebration

Chapter 17 Praying for Strength

Missing Person

Teardrops hit the dusty earth as a guttural moan breaks the stillness. In horror, I realize the sound is coming from me. It has been six months since I have seen my father. I miss him terribly. Now, my father is not a missing person in the traditional sense. I know exactly where he is. I know what happened to him. I know most of the answers to my questions. What I do not know is how to accept what happened and move on toward better things. He truly is not missing; he is always in my heart.

My father is dead. He passed away a mere six months ago, after a yearlong battle with an aggressive form of lymphoma. I know right where he is. He is in Heaven. His body is in a casket, sealed in a vault, and buried under six feet of sod-covered rocky earth. I know where he is. And I miss him. He runs a marathon through my mind on many days. I see pictures from the wake and the funeral slide show. I hear him talk to me in my memories. I see him holding the grandchildren, playing catch with me when I was younger, celebrating milestones with my mom. I see him sitting in his recliner, hoarding the remote, watching sports programs.

His memory stays in my mind, sometimes buried under more pressing matters, sometimes at the forefront of my day. I go to work with him on my mind. I watch athletic events and feel as if I can hear his comments after a foul as if he were speaking in my ear. I am always reminded of him when I visit our local community college. He spent the greater part of his forty year teaching and coaching career there. The swimming pool bears his name. A sign on the wall of the gym was placed in memoriam. While his body is absent, his spirit is always there. I can look at different areas of the gym and almost see him sitting there. He and my mom often attended the basketball games at the college, even after they retired from teaching there.

Family Tradition

My daughter, his first grandchild, continues the tradition of attending school at GSCC. She is part of the women's basketball team. I attend as many games as possible. In my mind, that is what my father would expect me to do. My daughter carries on the tradition of being a part of the action in the gym, but I am still sad. I know it is difficult for her as well. The signs that bear his name are impossible to ignore. How hard it must be for her, as she is surrounded by his name every day. She begins the third generation of our family to be associated with the college.

His memory weighs me down. Some days the weight is practically unbearable. Sometimes I feel haunted by the memories. While I do not want to forget them, I need the memories to recede so I can continue. I go through the motions of going to work, completing my duties, listening to others, but working like a zombie. Some days, I pray that no one asks me to complete any task out of the ordinary. I do not know that I could do it.

I cannot seem to shake the grief. I do not feel responsible for his death, but somehow, I feel like there is a connection that will not break. I find myself reliving the last days of his life. I cannot get those days out of my head. I know he suffered. I prayed that he would go easily, that he would not fight, that he would simply sleep and not wake. Those prayers were not answered in the way I hoped. Perhaps one day I will know the reason.

My father was a strong man, which is why watching him weaken and die was so difficult for my family. He was solid, a man's man, purely male. He was accustomed to having the women in the family take care of him. My mom, sister, and I always worshipped the ground he walked on. We did everything he asked and tried to please him. His compliments were like gold, and his praise was more valued than jewels. With him gone, we are all simply existing, complacent in our lives, waiting for there to be something more, some replacement, some reason to live. We know no replacement for him exists, but we wait for something, anything, to fill the void left by his death.

"Above the Grass"

I believe I am experiencing the phenomenon known as "survivor's guilt." I do not know if my mom and sister feel the same way, but I am forever scarred by the entire experience. I am distraught that he died and I am still alive. I know, logistically, that he should die first. He was the father and older. I realize that losing a parent is a rite of passage for most adults. Caring for an elderly or ill parent is far from unusual; in fact, it is now considered the norm. However, even knowing all these things, I feel guilt. Guilt that I could not provide more time for him, could not offer my children more experiences with him, could not cure him. I know, I know, I am not a doctor, or a magician, or in any way equipped to cure cancer. Why do I feel guilty that he died? I may never know.

All I can truly say is I know my mom, sister, and I did what we thought was best in caring for Dad. We made the trips to UAB; we got a second opinion at M. D. Anderson. Should we have tried somewhere else, too? I can't imagine that the results would be different, but how can I be so sure? I cannot; and that fuels the fire that is my guilt. I know my father wanted to live. When anyone asked how he was, he replied, "Above the grass." This three-word statement let us know how proud he was to be alive. He told the doctor many times that his only goal was to live.

One Million Dollars

Perhaps if we had traveled to Duke University, the Cancer Centers of America, or Mayo Clinic things would be different now. Our motto was "No Regrets" when it came to caring for my father. No stone was left unturned in our search for cancer care. My sister and I read everything we could find on how to help chemotherapy patients conquer the pain and sickness that come from the harsh poisons. We shopped at Whole Foods. We fed him vegetables from the garden, where we could control the amount of pesticides and fertilizers. We had friends who grew, picked, and prepared fresh green beans and brought them to the house many times just for Dad. He drank Boost, Ensure, and milkshakes with protein powder added. He faithfully took all his oral medications. We even considered the idea of using some natural remedies. We used hand sanitizer by the gallon. All possible disease precautions were taken and every far-fetched idea that might improve the quality of his life was endorsed, all to no avail.

I remember vividly my father's response to the question always asked by the doctors, nurses, and us as we left the hospital room. The question was, "Do you need anything?" His response was, "One million dollars." We would laugh at him and tell him we would be back with his money. Eventually he changed his request to two million dollars. I guess he realized parking fees at the hospitals in Birmingham and Houston would deplete his one million dollars quickly. Even when he was so tired and ill that he could not speak, if we asked what he needed, he would hold up two fingers to indicate two million dollars. He did not often ask for anything, preferring simply to take what was given and be happy. He loved vanilla ice cream and we often brought milkshakes and sundaes to him. He rarely, until the end, turned down ice cream or milkshakes. His motto was, "Ice cream goes with anything." Toward the end of his sickness, if he only felt like eating dessert, that is all he ate. Just about every dessert included ice cream. His second favorite was lemon icebox pie. Both of these treats were cool and probably cooled his mouth and throat. One side effect of chemotherapy is mouth sores.

Flair Hair

A few months into my father's journey through cancer, I had the opportunity to travel to Las Vegas, Nevada, with my husband and two other couples, to present at a conference. While there, I bought souvenirs for everyone in the family. My husband has a shaved head, and found a Flair Hair hat he wanted. Flair Hair is a visor with fake hair on top. Many colors and designs are available, but my husband opted for a realistic look. I decided that my dad, who had lost his hair to chemotherapy, should have a Flair Hair hat. How surprised and pleased he was to wear that hat. I really bought it as a joke, but he said the fake hair was very warm and kept the wind from cooling his head. Instead of wearing a toboggan, he began wearing his new hat every time he ventured outside. One of his greatest joys was to tip his hat to the ladies as he rode in his wheelchair through the hospital. The doctors, nurses, and others all laughed and joked about his "hair hat." In the chemotherapy infusion waiting room, he became something of a legend. Everyone wanted to see his hair hat. He was always quick to point out that it was a precious gift from his girls. My heart smiles when I think back to those days.

When hospitalization and chemotherapy treatments proved ineffective, my family made the decision to forego additional medical treatment. It was determined that no other options were available, so actually, the decision was already made. At that point, armed with the same diagnosis from two separate major hospitals, we discontinued medical treatment. The chemotherapy caused him to be ill for almost the entire week between treatments. What type of life was he actually living? We opted for quality of life over quantity of life. Was that the right decision? I guess we will always second-guess ourselves.

A few weeks before his death, Dad fully understood that nothing short of a miracle could cure him. His thoughts turned to sadness, as he realized that his time on Earth was limited. I remember sitting on the back porch with him and Mom, all of us lamenting the lack of options. I remember feeling stabbed in the heart when Dad stated, "I feel like everyone has given up on me." With no other treatment available, Dad's condition would not improve. In fact, at one point early in the summer, it was suggested that he would only have two weeks remaining to live. This prediction was inaccurate, but only by a few weeks. Things for my father only got drastically worse as the weeks progressed. No amount of prayer or care could change Dad's length of life. Even after numerous explanations, Dad still felt like there must be something, some treatment, some experimental drug, some chemo or radiation, some medicine, anything, that could help him. He knew he was dying and did not want to leave.

Guilt by Association

My emotional growth is stunted, stopped by the turn of events of the summer of 2013. My emotions are still raw. I hesitate to acknowledge any change, as I feel it would dishonor my father to have happiness and joy at this point. I cannot celebrate without thinking about what he is missing. I know in my heart that all is well with his soul, but perhaps, something is missing from mine. I rejoice that he is healed. I know he is well, celebrating in Heaven. I know that death is something that is a much harder journey for the living than the dead. In my mind, I acknowledge all these things. In my heart, I refuse to accept them. While I know that at some point, I must allow this grief to diminish, I fear that letting go of the trauma and sadness will tarnish the sacred memories I clinch tightly inside my mind. I will not take the chance of losing those precious memories. Perhaps I deserve the torture of remembering. Maybe, in some odd way, I feel responsible. I know that is preposterous. What could I have done to make him sick, or, for that matter, to make him well? The answer is nothing. The survivor's guilt in me still makes me question the events that happened. Did we do all we could? Absolutely. Was our best good enough? Not a chance. Is the guilt I feel real? Certainly.

We spent that last summer moving from the kitchen to the living room, from the bedroom to the back porch. We took short walks to the pier and the river in his backyard. We watched ESPN for hours on end. We walked through the remains of his garden, looking at the ruined tomatoes, the succulent blueberries, the sticky muscadines and scuppernongs, the "alleged" asparagus plants that never produced any product. The children took pride in picking the fruits and vegetables, but before long, the remains were only weeds and wormy fruits and vegetables. The selected produce was picked, cooked, and devoured, and all that remained were inedible items. Perhaps that is an analogy for our feelings of that summer. We try to remember as many of the wonderful times as possible and put the bad times in the trash as ruined.

Dad began to be more winded and require more rest. His walks became shorter until there were no more.

He was appalled to have to use a walker or wheelchair. How unfair—what this disease had done to my strong, athletic father. Only a few months before, he could still shoot free throws without missing. He would demonstrate different basketball plays. He was strong from farming and keeping his body fit. He lifted hay bales as though they were made of air. He carried two small grandchildren at once. But now, he had to be helped to stand. His appetite waned and his tastes changed. He tried so hard to eat. He knew he must eat to keep his strength, but his body rejected most food. His diet consisted of soft, bland items, and of course, ice cream or pie. Eventually, he could not eat.

Superhero

I remember the day we got him out of his bed, put him in a wheelchair, and rolled it up to the table. He would not open his eyes. He would follow instructions to open his mouth, and he would even take bites of eggs and grits. He drank a little juice from a straw. But he didn't open his eyes. He couldn't open his eyes. He was functioning as if asleep. His body and mind would not allow him to do any more than that. We put him back in the bed and sat at his side, realizing that what we had feared was happening now. We all sat at his bedside while my mom called the hospice nurse who confirmed our fears. "Seventy-two hours," she said with finality that I found hard to believe. "Usually, patients pass away within seventy-two hours from this point."

"She doesn't really know my father. He is not a regular patient. He is my dad. He is Superman. He is Iron Man, Captain America, the Hulk, and Batman all rolled into one human," I thought. "He will go through these seventy-two hours and prove them all wrong." Instead, I was drastically mistaken; three days later he was dead. The funeral is over and we are all moving along with our lives. The grief still envelopes me, surprising me--at times with tears, and at other times with rage. The grief is one extreme or the other; nothing in the middle. I am unsure about how to move past it. I'm afraid that if I move past the grief, I will lose part of my father, the part that I hold deep inside; the part that makes me so grateful to have known him, first as a father, later as a friend. I fear the unknown of letting go of the grief. What will happen to my memories? Will they become stagnant and faded over time or remain bright and joyous? Will I lose a part of me when I lose the last remnants of him? Pictures and memories are the only way, now, to document the man he was; the only way to preserve his spirit, his humor, his kindness. I am afraid to let go of the grief, because I fear it will be like letting go of the last piece I have of him. I will not let go. I cannot let go.

Pocketknives and the DMV

Everywhere I look, there are reminders of my father. Some are pleasant; some disheartening, some even a little funny, but most all of them are bittersweet. I see the horses at the barn. I watch my son use a pocketknife to cut hay string from bales of hay as he feeds the horses. My father did not leave the house without a pocketknife, even when he was ill. We buried him with his knife, because he would have been lost without it. Everything about the situation reminds me of my father. I hear Brandt tell me that Pop told him to "stay low" when he played on the line in football. I can see Brandt doing just that when he is on the field. He tells me after the game that he tried to do what his Pop said. I am glad Brandt remembered my father's words, but as he gets older, will his memories of Dad fade? Mine are still so fresh, even six months after his funeral. I probably remember more than I should.

I cannot bring myself to drive his red pickup truck. I know it is required for farm work, yet I have not found the courage within myself to actually sit inside the truck and crank it up. I know my mom and sister have both driven it, out of necessity. It is a Chevy four-wheel drive truck and my sister drove it during some recent snow and ice. My mom has driven it to care for the horses. I prefer to drive my Jeep and meet them. I have four-wheel drive as well, but the reality is I still see my father's silhouette when I look at his truck. This truck was the driver's education vehicle in our family. My daughter and son both learned to drive in this vehicle. My daughter, who now has her driver's license, was the first to drive it as an underage driver. My son, who is now thirteen, also took his turn driving it around the farm. My father always though the kids needed to know how to drive if an emergency ever occurred. I think he was right. I am thankful he took the initiative to teach them the basics. I am also thankful he gave them the memory of riding along with him in the infamous red truck.

One Day at a Time

I try to take each day as it comes, not worrying about what might happen, not stressing over the small things, but still, the guilt and doubt creep into my mind. I wonder how things might be different. I consider the feelings my sister, mother, and the grandchildren have. The children do not often express their grief—perhaps it is, for them, easier to process. The loss, while a direct hit to the family, is less for them, because they are more consumed with their personal daily schedules of school, athletics, part-time jobs, friends, and homework. Their free time is scheduled. My schedule is less defined. I work, sometimes watch ballgames, and then go home to prepare supper or do some laundry. I buy groceries, shop for clothes and shoes, and rent videos. I read, play computer games, check and respond to email, and post on social media. I sometimes visit with friends or maybe catch a show on television. My mind is, way too often, free to wander back to the grief that would consume me, if I let it. I obviously need more hobbies. My schedule is dynamic, changing every afternoon. There are no set rules about what I should do.

My family has survived these past months by simply soldiering on. We acknowledge the differences in our lives. We no longer share the spark that was our husband and father. Now, we just survive. There is less joy in living. Do not get me wrong. We still celebrate the accomplishments and joys of our children and grandchildren. We go out to eat. Mom attends grief share meetings with a few other widows. My sister and I have involved ourselves with the activities of our children and spending time with friends, many of whom have also lost a parent. We continue to live, but at this point, we do not thrive. We exist, but do not grow.

Times still exist when I awaken thinking I have overslept and it is time for my shift watching over my father. I jump up and start to prepare—then I remember. My time of watching him is done. There are no more days where I will have to set aside my schedule to care for him. Now, my personal schedule is the only thing I must complete. I have no medicines to give, no breathing treatments to administer, no chart to document everything. I have no reason to wake with a start. There is no rush to spend time with him. He is gone. Now, my only concern is if I can make time to visit his grave. I have my mom to care for, but she does not need the constant care my father required during his illness. She is self-sufficient but lonely. Maybe I can visit her today. I do not have to do so, but I enjoy our visits. I cannot imagine the pain she must be going through as her day is only about her. I have my husband, children, and work to fill my time. She does not have these things to occupy her any longer.

Everything Changes

I question my efforts to repair this hole in my heart. I feel this writing is cathartic for me. But what about everyone else? What does my mom do to express her sadness, her hurt, her pain? I do not know. I only know that she is sad. Her world has been turned upside down. For the year my father was sick, her job was mainly to take care of him. Now, he is gone and she has only herself to take care of. She has the house, the dog, and the horses. She has the cabin on the river. She has the farmland. Her time now consists of taking care of all these "things." At least it keeps her occupied. I do not know what her mental condition would be if she did not have ways to take her mind off the loss of her husband.

Mom suffers the most of all of us. Her soul mate of fifty years is gone. She had spent her life since college with my dad. Now, their marriage was not perfect. No marriages ever are, but they made it work. Her life is dramatically different. She went from being half of a very active couple, to being a caregiver, then to being a widow. For the past eighteen months, every day brought some new problem to conquer. So many things have happened in the six months that my father has been gone.

I will never forget the instant my mom realized, through the fog surrounding the evening of my father's death, that Dad was really, truly gone. We were gathering his clothes to take to the funeral home and debating what suit and tie my father should wear in the casket. My mom had chosen a suit Dad liked and she thought was handsome. Mom was placing the outfit together on the bed. She suddenly stopped, looked at my sister and me, and froze. The look that passed across her face was haunting. I see it in my dreams. It was as if the reality of his passing was affirmed in that instant. The look contained many emotions: loss, fear, anger, anguish, disbelief. My mom was confronted with her worst fear—being left alone. She had spent the past fifty years with my father. She rarely left his side after he became ill. Now, he was gone. The constant in her life for so long was gone. While she is not alone in her life, she is alone at her home.

Mom sleeps alone, in a cold, king-sized bed. There is no one she can put her cold feet on in the night. No one steals the cover. No one leaves socks on the floor. No one double-checks the door locks or turns on the alarm. No one fixes her a cup of coffee first thing in the morning. No one gets the mail or brings in the newspaper, or takes the trashcan to the street. Everything is now her responsibility. No one is around to do all the things my father did for her. He is not there to fill her car's tank with gas. He is not there to cut the grass, rake the leaves, and weed the garden. He is not around to wash the dishes after she fixed a meal. No one is there to replace a faulty washer on the kitchen faucet.

Dad is not there to tell her she is beautiful, or say he loves her, open her car door, or carry in the groceries. He is not there to hold an umbrella over her in the rain, or drop her off at the door before parking the car. He is not there to carry her packages when she is shopping and hold her purse as he waits for her to try on clothes. He is not there. He is not there. He is not there. There were so many things that my father did to help my mother. Now, he is not there. We are all lost without him, none more than Mom.

Cabin Fever

When my parents retired after forty years of teaching, they had plans to travel with friends, visiting places that time had not allowed them to visit before. They went to Branson, Missouri, took a cruise down the Mississippi River, and stopped to see the original Field of Dreams (built for the movie of the same name) in Iowa. They spent time with my father's niece and her husband in Panama City, Florida. They had a "supper club" with other couples and sometimes even went to the movie theater. They were often found watching athletic events together, from football games and volleyball matches in the fall, basketball in the winter, and to baseball, softball, and track in the spring. They watched the grandchildren's games, the local community college matches, and a nearby university's games as well. Holidays in warm weather meant barbeques at their cabin on the river. All the family attended, and usually brought other friends too. Spring and summer found them working in the yard gardening, visiting the horses or farmland, and then resting in the swing on the porch in the evening. They spent hours cleaning the cabin for summertime use. Many river parties, including holiday, birthday, reunion, and church, were held at the "cabin on the river."

Some friends have even lived in the cabin during times of home repair. One couple lived there during a transition into a new home. Another family lived there after a 2011 tornado destroyed their home. My folks rarely missed an opportunity to give of themselves in this manner. Their home was always open. My sister and I were encouraged to bring our families or friends over to share in the fun of living on the river. My sister and I coach and have each brought our teams to the river for cookouts. The cabin represents such fun times in the years my folks have lived there. We have spent countless hours there, swimming, riding jet skis and boats, fishing from the pier, cooking out, and enjoying each other's company. Now, the cabin seems different. Not physically different, but different in the fact that the man who loved it so is no longer around to enjoy it. He was the one who kept the minnows in the bucket for fishing.

He kept the rods and reels in good condition. He made sure there were adequate life jackets and tubes for riding the Jet Ski. Anytime the cabin was to be in use, he made sure there were plenty of chairs and tents available for all the guests. He put ice in the cooler to keep the drinks cool. He put umbrellas over the patio tables. Now, those things will have to be done by someone else. Maybe we took all he did for granted. I know I will surely miss him when summer rolls around and we have to remove the chairs from storage. We will have to clean them and possibly do some repair. Any other year, he would have already done those things in preparation. The physical work does not bother me. The heartache from missing him does.

Snowpocalypse

The weather in the South during the winter months is generally mild. We have an occasional cold front move through, bringing some freezing temperatures, but usually no snow or ice. This winter was an exception. We experienced a period of over sixty hours with subfreezing temperatures. Schools were delayed. Plumbing issues were rampant. Pipe insulation was sold out for miles around. During this cold snap, we had no snow, but, for us, extreme cold. We do not have appropriate clothing for wind chills below zero. We have relatively little practice driving on snow and ice, for times of such weather are few and far between. Unforeseeably, we have had the equivalent of two separate snowstorms already this winter season. Each brought closed roadways and schools. Kids played, drivers wrecked, and pipes burst. My mom and her dog were toasty warm during these times. My sister and I continued to check on her and even offered to bring her to our homes. She would not leave her house, for she worried about her dog and freezing pipes. My sister and

I were perfectly fine, playing in the snow with our children, drinking hot chocolate, and enjoying the family time. Mom was also fine, but nervous about being alone in such a situation for the first time since dad's death.

Everything worked out for the best, or at least, so we thought. After the snow and ice melted and a warming trend was on its way, my mom made her way to the cabin. Unfortunately, the cabin's pipes were old and did not fare well during the freeze. The pipes had burst and standing water was all over the kitchen area. This, added to a burst water heater, became Mom's latest headache to have to deal with. My father would have known exactly what to do, or who to call. Instead, Mom called her neighbors, Jason and Jennifer. Jason is quite mechanical, so he quickly came over to turn off the water and help dry the floors. The damage was done, and some of the hardwood floors were ruined. A portion of the flooring would have to be replaced, along with much of the pipe that ran under the cabin.

While I hate the fact that this happened, at least Mom has something to keep her busy. She has also chosen to remodel a portion of her home, as well, a plan that was hatched long before my father became ill. My sister and I joke with her that she is spending all our inheritance. However, we do understand her need for a change, especially a good, productive change.

Home is Where the Heart Is

My father died at home, in a hospital bed, in his and Mom's bedroom. He did not like hospitals and preferred, at all costs, to die at home. Regardless of the detriment to us, we followed his wishes. Actually, I think it made things easier, right up until his death. He was able to have many visitors, home-cooked meals, and his fifty-five inch television with the sound bar. He rested comfortably in his recliner, sat on the porch swing, and watched the fish jump out of the river water. He was able to relax and enjoy all the things he had spent his life working so hard to provide our family. His time was so limited after his retirement. He really did not have enough time to enjoy all he loved long enough.

Dying in a hospital room would have been a huge injustice to my father. He never enjoyed his hospital stays, but always made the best of them. He often got his days and nights mixed up when confined to a small room. I remember staying with him when he had the flu and was hospitalized for three days. He was restless, up and down, wanting to walk the halls all night. We made countless trips around the halls of UAB Hospital, stopping to look out windows and visit at the nurses' station. He was never rude or unruly, but always kind, chatty, and positive about his condition. He never met a stranger and often visited with the other patients when he felt well enough.

Immediately after my father's death, my husband, brother-in-law, and my daughter's boyfriend all went to work removing the hospital bed and other equipment from the bedroom. We did not want my mom to have to see those things. The reminder of the empty hospital bed would simply have been too much for any of us to endure. The suction machine, the oxygen tanks, the bottles of medicine were all harsh reminders of the thing we had lost. I did not want to see them and I know my mom would not want to see them either. When all those things were removed, the bedroom was returned to the way it had been just weeks before. Innocent bystanders viewing the room would not know the pain and misery suffered there, nor would they be able to acknowledge the moment the angels dove from Heaven to pluck my father's soul and leave only his broken body.

<u>"Where is Poppa?"</u>

When my father died, my niece Riley was about two and a half years old. Two memories of her insightfulness remain lodged in my memory. She, with the other three grandchildren, saw Dad's body the night of his death, when he was still in the hospital bed in the bedroom. The morning after Pop's death, Riley walked into his bedroom and immediately asked, "Where is Poppa?" I explained that Poppa was not with us anymore. She said, "Is he asleep?" Thinking that was as good an answer as any, I just replied, "Yes." I did not know how much she could process, and I did not want to upset her. She saw him again when he was in the casket at the wake. She wanted to pet him. Her father was holding her and she reached down to my Dad and ever so gently, patted his cool face. She loved her Poppa and was so kind and sweet to his body.

After the funeral, we ate lunch at the church. As she waited in line to fix her plate, Riley looked around the room at all the family, then looked at me and asked, "Where's Poppa?" The look on her face was one of curiosity. I know she did not know what had really happened. I know she just wondered where he was, since she, like us, had spent a great deal of time at his home. She knew we were all gathered there, but she did not really know why. She just knew Pop should be there too. I do not exactly remember what I said, but I think I just explained that Pop would not be with us anymore. He was gone to Heaven with Jesus. I suppose that satisfied her mind for the moment, for she then turned her attention to chicken fingers. The real test is keeping his memory alive for her in the coming years. I will often question her about Pop, just to make sure she remembers. I will bring up funny times with him that I remember her observing. She laughs and acts as though she remembers. I have videos of Riley and Ellie dancing in the living room with my father in the background watching and cheering for them. Those videos will be priceless to the girls as they get older. They are priceless to me now.

Much like Riley, I also have caught myself walking in Mom's house and having the words, "Where is Dad?" right on the tip of my tongue. Dad's recliner faces the front door, the entry point for everyone into the house. I walk in the house and the first sight I see is his chair. During his illness, the recliner was his throne. He rarely had to get up, for we all hovered around ready to fulfill his every whim. The end table beside his chair held the things that were important to him: the television and cable remotes, the daily newspaper, a farm magazine, and a glass of lemonade or sweet tea. I was so used to seeing him sitting or napping in that chair. It is now difficult for me to see his chair, empty, without wanting to ask where he is. Then I remember, and the grief comes back, crushing me inside. I remember, and wonder how I could ever have forgotten. I remember, and now, I cannot forget.

Holiday Heartache

So many things are different for all of us. My mom is no longer part of the "supper club" because she refuses to attend and be a "third wheel." She would not go without my father. Her activities are limited to doing things with our families and spending time with her widowed friends group. She will still lunch with her favorite girlfriends but does not attend "couple" events. She has gradually changed where she sits at church, because she and my father once sat on a particular pew. I find it difficult to remain on that pew now myself. She is learning how to play Mah Jongg, a tile game, with her widows group, but she does not often play cards, for the memories might be too strong. My father was a well-known cheater when he played cards. Everyone wanted to be his partner in Rook games, because he had tricks that would help his team pull out a win, even with a bad hand of cards. He could perform card tricks by the dozen, but rarely explained the process to work the trick. I remember when my son showed an interest in a magic kit. My father thought it was a grand idea, and took that opportunity to show my son some of the card tricks he knew. Imagine the delight of my (then) five-year-old son.

My mom, sister, and I have had to experience many events without our father. We have attended church, athletic events, and ceremonies. We have survived many of the major holidays in which our entire family should be present. We have made it through Thanksgiving, Christmas, and Dad's birthday. Let me be brutally honest: Thanksgiving was the first and probably the toughest for me, followed closely by Christmas. Thanksgiving involved having my father's relatives at my mom's home and celebrating both the Thanksgiving meal and a fish fry. My daughter was not there for she was on a trip with her basketball team. It was the first holiday when people were missing. It was horrible. I had suggested that my mom, sister, and I, and our families take a trip somewhere so we could not be forced to go through the motions as if everything were normal. I thought we should travel to Florida to watch my daughter's basketball tournament. However, my suggestions were to no avail and instead, plans were in place for a reunion with my father's family at Mom's home. We did not go anywhere and it was, at some points, torture for me. Now do not get me wrong, I enjoyed spending time with relatives we only see occasionally, but I simply did not like the idea of all of us gathered and my father gone. The memories of previous holidays, weighed heavily on my mind. I can only assume my sister and mom felt the same emotions.

That holiday started a six-week period of celebration that was, at best, difficult, and at worse, disabling. Thanksgiving was followed by Christmas, New Year's Day, and Dad's birthday. Each of these days and seasons has special meaning to us. Now these times are tainted. Some of the joy is gone. Some of the fun is lost. Thanksgiving led into the Christmas season, which meant Christmas parties and school plays. My family watched my niece's preschool program and took them all out to eat. My dad would have been there if he had been alive. My sister and I had Christmas parties at work. My mom attended our Christmas program at my school. I was so pleased to see her there and I was glad she ventured out. We all did some Christmas shopping, but it felt odd to leave my father off my shopping list. For all these years, my sister and I have purchased gifts for my dad. Now there was nothing to buy. My father usually gave my sister or me money and asked us to purchase something for my mom. He liked to buy her small things from our local trade day or flea market. I cannot tell you how many knick-knacks he had purchased her over the years. She always received the most gifts on Christmas morning. This Christmas was different.

Our usual Christmas rituals for my immediate family include a service at church on Christmas Eve night followed by a movie at the theater and then a meal at Waffle House. Normally, no eating establishments remain open after the movie except Waffle House (All Star Special Breakfast). After the meal, we return home and wait for Santa to visit. The next morning, the children see their surprises from Santa and we all exchange gifts. We go to Mom's house for a delicious brunch around ten on Christmas morning. We eat a fantastic meal, with our tradition of an egg casserole, cinnamon rolls, biscuits, cheese grits, and assorted breakfast meats. When the dishes are done, usually by the men of the family, the children dispense the gifts from under the tree to each recipient. The children begin the gift opening and chaos ensues. There are always so many gifts for everyone, and the living room is filled with shards of Christmas wrapping paper ripped from the packages. The cleanup takes longer than the actual opening of the presents. Mom insists on saving the bows and boxes for reuse. We usually spend the day with my parents, then go to my in-laws home for supper and more gift exchanging. It is normally an exciting day with great food, fun, and fellowship with our families.

This year, however, was a bit different. My sister and I were certain that we did not want my mom to be alone when she woke on Christmas morning. After our church service and a Waffle House visit on Christmas Eve, we all went to Mom's house to spend the night. I must say, all of us crowded into her house made for interesting sleeping arrangements. Instead of dreaming of sugarplums and Santa, the theme of the evening was insomnia.

This is terrible to say, but no one wanted to sleep in the bed with Mom because she snores. I mean really snores. Like, rattle the house snores. (We have since convinced her to partake in a sleep study and she now has a BiPap machine to help with her sleep apnea.) My sister and her baby girl slept in the middle room. My daughter and niece slept in the upstairs bedroom. My son slept on the couch. My husband and I stayed at the cabin in the backyard. It was an interesting set-up for sure. I am not sure if anyone really slept much. The kids were all excited about Santa coming and we never sleep as well when we are not in our own beds. I feel certain that my mom did not sleep well. I do not think she was sleeping well anyway, but when you add a houseful of guests, especially the daughters who do not sleep well either, it is basically a recipe for disaster. My sister and her girls got up early and went home to see what Santa brought them. My kids enjoyed their Santa gifts at Mom's house. We got started cooking and before we knew it, everything was ready. The food was delicious, but my father was not there. The gifts were exciting, but my father was not there. The children played with their new toys, but my father was not there. My mom really liked the Keurig and assorted K Cups I got her, but my father was not there. I was glad to get a few new things, but my father was not there. Regardless of the fun we had, nothing was as great as previous Christmases because my father was not there. We had no trade day gifts for my mom, and there were no jokes about Dad getting underwear and socks. Things will never be the same, because my father was not there. Holidays in general are tolerated, not celebrated, because my father will not be there.

Cemetery Celebration

Dad's birthday was in January. He would have been seventy-five. The day was cold, rainy, and dreary, much like our moods on that terrible day. We visited his grave and tied balloons around the flower arrangement. Mom, Kim, and I all cried. We prayed for us, the remains of our little family. We prayed for guidance, strength, and peace. We walked back to our respective vehicles, drying our eyes. As I got in the car, I noticed my jacket was wet with rain and tears. The tears were not just mine. The jacket held the tears of my mother and sister. The jacket held the grief that we all felt, and still feel. The jacket held the love that we all wanted so desperately to give to my father, but he was not there to receive it.

I remember the thoughts I had after leaving the cemetery that day. How could I possibly ever be strong enough to hold Mom and my sister up during their grief and sorrow? I feel as though I should be their protector. My father is not here. The job is now mine. I wonder if the responsibility on me is too great, too pressing, too much for me to bear. Who is going to hold me up? My nature is one of giving. I am accustomed to doing for others. Sometimes I wonder when things will be done for me—then I remember all the kindnesses of others while my father was sick and since. I cannot dwell in this self-pity. I must move on. The time for my meltdown will be later, when I feel like the others can tolerate life without a back-up plan.

Valentine's Day was especially hard for my mom and my sister. Thankfully, each had various events to attend, including a basketball game at the local high school. That kept their minds, somewhat, off the more pressing problem of vivid memories. The day was made more difficult for my mother, because my dad always made sure she had a gift. While they did not exchange any large gifts, Mom always received flowers from Dad. This year, I made sure she got some flowers. I know it was not as nice as getting a gift from my dad, but I wanted her to know I love her. I know she knows I love her, but I did not want her to go through the day without knowing how often I think about her. I hoped just a token gift from me would encourage her.

Praying for Strength

Recently my daughter's basketball team made it to the ACCC (Alabama Community College Conference) tournament. The tournament was played at Wallace State Community College in Hanceville, Alabama. My mom and I made the hour and a half trip two times during the week. While I was excited for the team to play, (and end up runner-up in the state championship) it was a difficult place for me to be. The last time I had attended a game there was the year before, when the GSCC men's basketball team was in the tournament. My father had been there with us, certainly not well, but not as ill as other times. He had eaten popcorn, cheered for the team, and talked basketball with the fans around us. After the game, we stopped for a meal at the local McDonald's restaurant. He had eaten well and seemed to have a great time, even though the team we were rooting for lost the game. The trip this year was difficult. He was not there to cheer, argue debatable calls, or eat a Big Mac.

My mother and I found ourselves talking on the trip home about how unfair life seems. As I drove, I had to force myself to concentrate on the road. I wanted to just put my head down and sob about the events that took my father away from us. As we talked, the tears rolled down my face. The lines on the roadway blurred. I took deep breaths to calm my nerves. I could not look at my mom. I focused only on keeping the vehicle on the road. My mom cried, too. The two of us together talking about my father was obviously a recipe for disaster.

Life is unfair. My dad did not drink or smoke, kept himself in good shape, ate whatever healthy meals my mom prepared, and took any medication as prescribed. He was a good man, one who helped others, both financially and physically. We talked about his love for farmland, livestock, and his grandchildren. I reminded Mom about his strong love for her. His last spoken words were to tell her he loved her. Such is the devotion of a great man. Dad was a friend to many and a foe to few.

During the ride home, Mom and I both questioned if things would ever be back to normal. I do not think that will ever happen. So many things are different now. We have decided to plant some of the farmland with pine trees to harvest in later years. It is a way to keep the land in use, without having livestock, which requires feeding and care. We have decided to sell my father's boat, the one he used to cruise the river. The motor needs some work and none of us wants the responsibility of being the boat captain. We will simply enjoy the Jet Ski and possibly purchase another one. Things are so different. I do not know how to adequately explain all the changes since Dad's death. I now refer to the time since his death as "the new normal."

I remember the little things about him. I remember his patience. I remember his humor. I remember how he could make me feel that everything would eventually be just fine. I remember that he took my side when I felt I had been wronged. He had the ability to make the things I worried about seem inconsequential. I wish he were here now to take away my worries. Perhaps I should take a lesson from him. While my concerns are slowly changing, I still miss my father and wish he were with us, healthy and complete. As much as I miss him, I know that I have no choice but to continue with the daily existence that I call life. The rainy season we are experiencing has lost some of its stormy power and eventually, just maybe, the sun will shine for my family again. As the rain continues, I pray for strength.

Book Three

Forever I Grieve: Praying for Peace

An adult daughter faces her hardest test after the loss of her father to an aggressive form of lymphoma. She learns to accept the loss and deal with his absence through prayer and spiritual discovery. This is the final step in her journey from her father's diagnosis to death. The story becomes her own journey, no longer based strictly on her father.

Table of Contents

Chapter 1—Ain't No Mountain too High for Him

Chapter 2—I'm a Believer

Chapter 3—Help Me Hold On

Chapter 4—Journey Back to Joy

Chapter 5—Prayer Priorities

Chapter 6—Clichés are Blasé

Chapter 7—What I Meant to Say Was…

Chapter 8—Singing Through the Pain

Chapter 9—Believe Me, Mary Already Knows

Chapter 10—Small Town Success

Chapter 11—Six Years More

Chapter 12—Double Vision

Chapter 13—Timing is Everything

Chapter 14—Sweet Summertime Blues

Chapter 15—<u>In-Law Illness</u>

Chapter 16—<u>Platitudes of Gratitude</u>

Ain't No Mountain too High for Him

Sometimes we do not realize the plan God has for us until we have struggled through the valley and returned to the mountain top. Only in hindsight can we see and appreciate the things God does to make our lives easier. It is only now, many months after my father's death, I can objectively look at his journey from diagnosis to death and feel more sweetness than sorrow, more admiration than anger, and more blessings than bitterness. I can finally acknowledge that as terrible as this journey became, my spirit was not crushed and my faith remains, stronger than ever.

It is what it is. This too shall pass. Everything will be okay. There is nothing I can do to change things. These are mantras that I have continuously reminded myself of daily. I feel helpless. I can do nothing; no action, no works, say no words, that will provide comfort or peace. I must accept the fact that I can do nothing. Helplessness is not a feeling that I have often experienced. I have always lived life as though I could conquer the world. Nothing was impossible—until now.

My father is dead, and one of the two constants is my life is missing. My mom remains, but she is consumed with her own version of grief. She is unavailable to help me deal with my grief. I am scared, lonely, unsure, afraid, insecure, frightened. I am alone. I have never faced a situation that offered absolutely no method to the madness. Maybe I am mad and this is how I show it. My family is broken. Our only recourse is to pray for repair. Nothing will completely mend our brokenness. We may be glued back together, but the cracks to our façade remain visible. I pray these cracks fade away over time.

I'm a Believer

I am a Christian. I believe completely in the Bible and in the fact that God has created me in His image and His son, Jesus, died on a cross at Calvary to cleanse my soul and make me pure. I believe that I am forgiven of my sins if I accept Jesus as my Savior, believe that He died for me, and confess my sins. I strive to live a life that is pleasing to God. I pray daily that my actions will reflect positively on Him and that I may be used as a vessel to spread His word. Every day I live, I fail. I sin. I am far from perfect. I struggle. I like to attempt to solve the problems of the world on my own, thinking that I know best.

Obviously, I do not know best. With the loss of my father, the insulated bubble I live in has lost some of its air. Things are so different, odd, troubling. I found (and still find) myself praying, weeping, struggling, with death. I know I cannot change anything, but some days I wish I had that power. I am the protector now, the one who takes the responsibility for my mother and sister. Now, I have my own family to protect as well, but I think of my mom and sister as alone and heartbroken. Perhaps I am wrong. I know they are both Christians, as well, and perhaps their faith is stronger than mine. I have not lost any of my faith. Instead, I believe this crisis, this crumbling of my spirit, this feeling of insecurity, has served to make my faith much more steadfast.

Help Me Hold On

I read a blog not long ago that addressed the feeling of being overwhelmed with sadness and strife. I do not remember the author's name, but I will never forget the opening statement of the blog. The title was along the lines of "God will never give you more than you can handle." The author went on to say she did not believe that to be true. She stated that nowhere in the Bible does God promise only good times. God will give us seasons of change, despair, anguish, and grief to help us fully rely on Him and His promises. This was indeed a needed wake-up call for me. While I think I had been moving toward the direction of again, fully trusting in God's plan and decisions for both my father and me, these words struck a chord in my heart. I read the blog again. Then I read the blog again. The words came alive as I reread them.

Basically, the blog suggested that God gives us difficult times and troubles in order to bring us closer to Him. I think it is the old adage of breaking the spirit in order to have obedience. I know I had chosen, on my own, to selfishly think my ways of dealing with the situation were the best, or only way. I had not necessarily obeyed the directions that God had provided for me. I wanted to grieve in my own way, suffer in the loss, exalt the pain, as though I was the only one who had ever felt such anguish. God used the blog to show me the error of my ways. God will, without a doubt, give us more than we are prepared to handle, in order to bring us back to completely trusting Him and learning to depend on Him as our source of strength. God will break us, then build us back as He desires. I withheld parts of my grief from Him, like He didn't already know. I thought I could control my destiny, make my own decisions, harness my anger at the situation. Reading the blog helped me make the decision to surrender my entire being to Him, again. No matter how angry, confused, or upset I was that my father suffered and died a terrible death, I now realize that the plan for my dad was in place long before I came along. I could not change it. I could not alter any part of it. No amount of prayer, tears, or curses would make a difference. God was not surprised that my father died and arrived in Heaven. God used my father's death to draw me closer toward accepting the plan He has for me.

Now, I have always considered myself one of God's children, and a fighter for Him, but the death of my father had left me so consumed with my own grief, pain, and despair, that at times, I refused to listen to the things God was trying to tell me. I never questioned my belief in God, I simply chose to walk my own path, and listen to my own understanding. How wrong I have been. I did not consciously turn away from God, but I allowed my grief to overshadow the plans I know He holds for me.

God has a plan for each of us. Whether we choose to follow that plan is our choice. I have chosen selfishly, and the resulting grief has been, partially, of my own making. I have not given it to Him, but I have hoarded the loss in my heart, thinking I could somehow, survive such a terrible loss simply through my own strength. Even the strongest people among us will have times when they are weak, when they fall, when life causes them pain. Even when tears rolled down my cheeks, I felt strong. I did not have a choice, or so I thought. I did not want to let go of my own strength and allow God to be the strength that my family so desired. I wanted to be that pillar. I wanted to be that rock. I wanted to be the one with all the answers. I was wrong. I am not strong enough on my own. I cannot provide adequate comfort for myself; why did I ever think I could be a comfort to someone else? I am only as strong as my God allows me to be.

Matthew 11:28 of the Bible (New English Translation) states, "Come to me, all you who are weary and burdened, and I will give you rest." God says He will hold our burdens, however, we must choose to hand them over to him. When we hold our burdens tightly in our closed fist, we are, by our own choice, deciding that our way is better than God's way. We decide that our decisions are better, our choices are better, our judgment is better. None of these options is actually true. Our best, and only option, in times of strife and struggle is to give our burdens away. If we give our problems to Him, He will take them, solve them, or destroy them. We can rest assured that nothing is out of the realm of God's possibility. God will take my burdens and allow me some recourse from the weariness that invades my days. He will let me recover from my wounds, if I turn my troubles over to Him. He will be my rock--my sword and shield in times of battle, even if the battle is within me. I know that the battle is already won, if I humble myself and expose my entire broken soul to Him.

I know this solution sounds easy, but the reality of it is not. It is difficult to turn loose of things we love. Some of us are control freaks. Some of us like to micromanage. Sometimes, we become so consumed with our problems and concerns that we fail to realize the larger picture. We only see what we want to see. We face times of trouble in all areas of life. Sometimes we lose our focus on what really matters—eternity. We place so much emphasis on the things of this world that our views are often blurred by what we decide is important. We refuse to look beyond the present, never envisioning anything past surviving today. Our lives are filled with sorrow, tragedy, and despair, laced with joy and exuberance, all for a reason. The reason for these changes is simple—to glorify God. When we accept God as our Savior, we know that a place far beyond anything we can imagine waits for us. We suffer through trials and tribulations as a means to an end. The end for those who die is Heaven. Those who remain behind must face the despair that comes from the loss. In order to recover from the loss, the burden of hurt must be given to God.

Journey Back to Joy

It is difficult for me to trust. In order for us to fully trust that God knows what He is doing, we must put aside our human desires and beliefs and place all our wants, fears, and insecurities in Him. We open our hearts to hurt, complications, despair, and sorrow. We must first experience an action, any action, which causes us to fail—to be broken—to have our perfect human world destroyed. We can offer our imperfect selves to God, and be assured that He will make us whole again. We must choose to place our burdens on Him, realizing that our human experience is limited. Based on this, it is not possible for us to be equipped or prepared to deal with things or experiences that cause us pain. When we turn to God, we may still experience loss, pain, and fear, but we are not alone in our journey. He travels with us, through every valley, to the pinnacle of every mountain. He holds my hand and guides me through all my travels. He is my escort through every situation, both good and bad, and extends his arm for me to grasp when needed.

My God is always with us, even if we do not acknowledge His presence.

I believe that God has given me the gift of writing in order to grieve. Writing allows me to express my thoughts and possibly, provide some comfort to others who may feel disappointment, anguish, or despair. While I absolutely despise the fact that writing comes from such terrible times, I acknowledge that all good things come from God. I did/do not know His plan. I only know that the death of my father left me with such a desire to write, that I had no other choice but to break out a pen and paper. I felt compelled to write. I still do. I am not sure why God gave me this desire now. Perhaps He recognized my need to vent, my need for understanding, my need to slice open the confines of my heart and let the words flow freely. Perhaps this need to write is part of God's plan for me. I do not know what the future holds, but my God knows that plan.

Because the words are flowing so easily, I can now learn to accept and move on with my life. I will never forget the way I have felt for over eighteen months, especially the last months of my father's life and the immediate months following his death. I refuse to forget. I know I cannot change the course of his life, but I have placed all the memories, both good and bad, in my heart. The problem exists when I choose to let the horrible memories outshine the beautiful ones, when I focus on his death, not his living. I cannot let this grief envelop me and change my disposition from fun and happy to sad and depressed. I will still cry. I will still visit my father's grave. I will still tear up when I think about the losses my children and nieces face without my dad. Writing has not been some type of magical, immediate cure. It is a process; a process to understand; a process that exacerbates my return to the fold as a child of God; an ever-changing process, which will cause me to reexamine, and possible reevaluate, my life and direction.

Sometimes God uses an unexpected moment to get our attention. God gives us reminders of His love and uses, we think, normal circumstances to make us realize He is always looking out for us. A friend of mine,

Shelly, is the Children's Ministry Director at our local church. She has volunteers who help her have children's church service each Sunday on a rotating basis, but Shelly usually schedules my friend Kim and me on the same day. Once, Shelly had to be absent so we took over the entire children's church program for the day. I read the lesson and the kids worked on their Bible verse for the week. We worked on coloring sheets and word find papers and played a game. At the end, Shelly had left another Bible story for me to read and a stone for each child to take home as a reminder. I do not know if the children really got the story, but I certainly did. I had one of those moments that you know God has designed exactly for you.

The story was one about Joshua. He led a group of people through the Jordan River. The river was full. It was not an empty riverbed. In order to get the people across, God directed Joshua to follow His plan. One man from each of the twelve tribes was to carry a stone to make a monument. The waters were parted and the group was able to pass through without danger. The monument was designed to be placed where all could see it and know that the hand of God was upon the people, just as Moses has said.

At the conclusion of reading the story, I gave each child a stone, (much like a marble) to represent the stones of the monument. I said to all the children, "This stone represents the presence of God that helped his followers make it through dangerous areas of the world. God does the same for us. This stone means that God will be with you through everything, just like He was with the people as they crossed the Jordan. God will help you go through, across, or around anything that troubles you. He is always in control."

As I finished saying these words, I realized that God had made things work out for me to be in children's church that day and have to share that story. I know He meant for me to hear the words and put a stone in my own pocket. I know, without a doubt, that God had his hand on the schedule of my friends, Shelly and Kim, and He made it all work out for His good. I still have the stone. I carry it in my pocket every day and when I reach in my pocket I stop and think about how God is always in control. It has taken me quite a long time to accept, fully, that He has the answers, not me. I touch the stone and am immediately taken back to the moment in children's church when I realized that I, not the children, was having a God moment. I thought He was using me as a worker for the children. Actually, He was using the children and their special service to work on me.

Prayer Priorities

When my father died, my family turned to our faith. Now, do not think that we had been absent from our faith. That is not what I mean. What I mean is, we became almost completely dependent on our faith to help us survive the terrible days immediately following my father's death. Throughout his sickness, we had often asked for prayer. Whenever he had to have a procedure completed, we asked for the prayers of our church family, Facebook friends, and co-workers. We placed our father's name on various church prayer lists, posted prayer requests on social media, and asked everyone we knew to keep our father and our family covered in prayer. We prayed for good test results, confident doctors, easy procedures, and no sickness with chemotherapy treatments. In an odd juxtaposition, my faith was stronger when my father was alive and hurting than when he was dead and buried. Perhaps the idea of him living, beating the cancer, gave me a tighter grasp of my faith. In all things, we prayed. We prayed for healing, a miracle, and finally, I prayed for his death. Yes, you read that right. I prayed for him to die.

My prayers changed as his prognosis worsened. Instead of praying for healing, instead of praying for his strength, for his body to heal, my prayers changed to focus on his death. I prayed he would sleep and in that slumber, fail to wake again. I prayed for a peaceful death—no fighting death, no trying to stay for our sake, no heroics of any sort. I prayed for my mom, my sister, the grandchildren. For all of them, I prayed for strength, peace, and the ability to remember the good and forget the bad. I wanted my father to pass into Heaven without fanfare—simply going to sleep or passing into a coma—escaping the constant pain that plagued his body.

You may question why I prayed for his death. Perhaps part of it was selfishness. I had almost reached the limit of my tolerance for watching him waste away from his illness while trying to hide his pain. He did not verbally complain, but when he thought no one was watching, or when he was asleep, he moaned, almost subconsciously. The pain he felt was real and deep, but he was too strong to let us see him hurt. I knew he hurt. I understood that his generation was one that did not show pain or weakness. I knew he would not express his pain until he could stand it no longer. This is the man who never complained. This is the man who once broke his cheekbone while at the farm and finished unloading hay before coming home, showering, and then driving himself to the hospital. When I asked why he finished the chores, he replied, "The cows still have to eat." That story exemplifies the strength of the man.

When people would ask how they could pray for us, I would respond that I wanted them to pray for healing, a working treatment plan, or no sickness. After a while, that changed and I began to ask them to pray for an easy death for him. Some people looked at me with curiosity. Dad always said he wanted to die in his sleep, instantly, with no pain, no trouble to anyone, nothing for anyone to have to deal with. Maybe that was his wish, but it was not in God's plan for him.

In retrospect, I believe the prayers for my father's healing were heard and answered by God. They were not answered in the way I wanted, but they were answered nonetheless. My father is healed. He lives in a place more beautiful than anything my mind can imagine. He has a full head of shiny white hair. His knees are free from arthritis. Dad's lungs are clear and the masses filling his body have disappeared. He is healed, and now his body is in the most pristine form ever, the true likeness of God. His healing is an answered prayer, even if the answer did not come soon enough for my liking. Who am to I question God's timing? Again, God was not surprised to see my father in Heaven. Instead, He was waiting to welcome my father, to see him as His child, to direct my dad to his reward (which I can only hope included a basketball court).

Clichés are Blasé

Even before Dad's death, the platitudes started coming from our friends. They were certainly well intentioned, but the words were not comforting. We would hear things like, "If God brought you to it, He will bring you through it," and "Let go and let God." After his death, those clichés changed to things like, "Your dad is in a better place" and "It is all in God's plan." I know the words were spoken with love, but at that time, I was not ready to slide up next to God and be His best friend. I was mad: mad at God, mad at the situation, mad at myself, and mad at everyone else, especially my friends whose fathers were still living. I know the anger is a part of the process of accepting death, but at that point I was unable (or unwilling) to deal with the death and all the emotion that surrounded it.

Another phrase I heard was, "It's not fair." That statement brought full agreement from me. It was not fair. It was not fair to my mom, to me, to my sister, to the grandchildren. It was not fair to my father's sister, nieces, and nephew. Nothing about the entire year-long episode was fair. My family, as well as our community, is better off for knowing my father, but his loss left us reeling. From my Biblical understanding, I know that God is not to be questioned. I know that I should not ask why my father, such an outstanding man, was taken from us in such a manner. I have heard all the ideas about how Heaven needed another angel and God had a job for him to do. I suppose those things are comforting in certain ways. I imagine that my father might be the guardian angel who protects the grandchildren. Quite possibly, God's basketball team needed a coach. Maybe he is in charge of Heaven's version of March Madness (somehow I think God's team wins). I do not know, and will not know until I reach the Pearly Gates myself, but I do like to imagine that God had an important job for my father, probably not as important as praising Him, but still, one of great distinction and honor.

What I Meant to say Was…

Now that I have been in the situation, I realize the best things I heard were, "I'm praying for you" and "I'm sorry." Nothing was going to change the situation, especially the common phrases said to those who suffer. I know that I am guilty of saying the same things to others in that situation, simply because I did not realize the effect of the words. I did not know the emotions passing through the living after such a death. I know that words can have a profound effect on people—I mean, I teach English for a living. I, of all people, should know the power of words to provide pleasure or pain.

I did not. I did not realize the power that these few words, uttered together during a hug, held over me. I was not aware of the emotions that formed such peaks and valleys in my soul. I had absolutely no idea of the feelings I may have caused in those who heard me speak the same words, "It is all in God's plan." How could I have been so blind (or deaf) to the power and passion of such a phrase? How could I, the English teacher, be so unaware of such power? How was it that the thought had never crossed my mind before? In all the times that I have comforted friends who were suffering losses, why had I never stopped to consider the impact of that string of six words? Oh, the guilt and shame I feel now. I had assumed, wrongly, that my friends who were devastated at a loss would find comfort, a sense of peace, some form of rest and reassurance in the phrase. Now, I know better. I prefer to say the things that gave me peace.

Believe me when I say that words, in some cases, are just words. They are said more for the speaker than the listener. The speaker does not often know what to say, and there is safety in throwing God into the conversation. While I am not saying the religious references do not help anyone, I will let the one who grieves take the lead in such things. I will say, "I am sorry," and hope that does justice to the situation.

Singing Through the Pain

When my father was in his final moments of life, I sang to him. I have a talent for singing that I do not use often enough. I have sung at church, in programs, and in the car. I have performed at weddings and funerals. I have sung to embarrass my children and touch the souls of those hungry for a message from God. I sang in community productions as a child, and with my husband at our own wedding. Singing to my father was my way of connecting with him in the crux between life and death. I sang an old song, now performed by Selah, about the Lord holding the hand of the one who wanted to be taken to Heaven. I pray he heard me. I hope he understood that I was giving him permission to go. I hope he knows that as much as I wanted him to stay, I even more desperately, wanted him to go.

For me, both during my father's illness and after his death, music provided great comfort. I have made playlists with songs that bring me peace. I listen to them whenever I feel worried or shaken and I want to speak to my father. Many of the songs I enjoy are the old hymns

121

from the Baptist church hymnals. I remember my grandparents listening to some of the same music when I was younger. My mother and her brothers and father would stand around a piano and sing while she played. These moments come alive to me when I hear the music. Maybe that is why I feel a sense of peace while listening to these hymns.

Many of Selah's songs have become staples in my playlists. The group is comprised of two men and one woman and the harmonies between them are fantastic. They take traditional music and give it an upgrade to a more upbeat tune, or a downgrade, to an acoustic or acapella selection. Either way, their music soothes my weary soul. Point of Grace is another group who provides music for relaxation. Three women anchor the group and provide delicious harmony through their original music. Casting Crowns is a third group that gave me some peace during the whole ordeal. When we were traveling to Houston for my dad's second opinion, I used the music on my phone and CD's to provide entertainment. Thirteen hours is an awfully long drive. I listened to almost every CD I had in the car, but still found myself drawn to a few of Selah's songs. I realize now that they were all based around the idea of fighting the good fight, making the best of the situation, turning things over to God, and continuing to honor the name of Jesus. While I sang the songs then, I did not really allow the meanings to penetrate my soul. Since dad's death, I take great comfort in the music that touches the innermost part of me. I listen closely and find myself mirrored in the lyrics of many songs. Singing with these groups in the car, as I drive to work, run errands, and go about my day allows me to focus not on just my grief, but also on my salvation. I am slowly allowing myself to think about singing with joy again.

Believe Me, Mary Already Knows

About two months after my father's funeral, I was asked to sing at the funeral of a man who had once been my church youth choir director. Another choir member was joining me for a duet. The funeral was another bittersweet moment. I did not think I could actually sing at a funeral so soon after my father's death. We met early to practice and sang a newer version of "Amazing Grace." While I loved the song before, I find it difficult to listen to it now. I had one of my father's handkerchiefs in my pocket to provide me with the strength to sing. I had taken it from his armoire and held it to wipe my tears at Dad's funeral. I refused to wash it because it had a certain scent that I associated with my father. I held that handkerchief tightly. I squeezed it as I sang and tears rolled down my cheeks. I could not look at the family. It was too soon. I wanted to be done. I was not totally comfortable there, but I had promised the family I would honor their loved one's request. When the song was complete, I breathed a sigh of relief. I had complete the task and survived. Now, I realize that God had placed this family in my path over twenty years ago in order for them to encourage me to sing after my father's death. After that day, singing became easier. I thought I might actually sing again, for pleasure.

So I did. I sang two selections in a Christmas program where I teach. One song was particularly moving because it often brings people to tears. I will practice on stage in the days before the program, and this year, I asked some retiring teachers to come listen so they would be prepared for the actual program performance. Ordinarily I will make a joke about the crying before I begin the song, but this year the performance was more difficult. My father had recently passed, my mother and son were in the audience, and my emotions were running a little high as we approached the holidays. Remember, this was during the six-week period of my gloom and doom. I sang the song, and almost had to stop and gather myself. Teachers were crying, my mom was beaming with pride, and I could not stop thinking that just a year ago, my only concerns were getting the presents wrapped in time for our gatherings. I made it through, but immediately had to have a Diet Dr. Pepper (the drink of champions). The blessing of singing is one I had sorely missed. Perhaps I will take the opportunity to sing in public again.

Small Town Success

You may be confused as to why and how our family is so close. We live in a small town and know just about everyone here. My sister and I are teachers at the school we graduated from; I teach at the middle school; she teaches at the elementary school. We both coach; I coach cross country (running) and previously coached volleyball, while she coaches cheerleading. We attend almost every athletic event that happens at the school. Our children go to these schools. We are products of our hometown. We live nearby our mom and often spend time together as an extended family. Our parents' home is located on a river, and we enjoy spending time with our friends and family there. My father and mother both taught at our local community college. He also coached and was athletic director there. Our parents were both well-known supporters of the community and schools. While my father's death was difficult for our family, it was also a blow to the entire community.

When I think about it, what could be a more important job on Earth than being a loving husband and father? My mom had a husband who was her perfect match. He was patient and relaxed while she was all bustling and business. He washed the dishes when she cooked. He did for her as a husband should do for his wife, and the love of his life. She, in turn, played the part of the ultimate companion and coach's wife. My father had the perfect wife for him. She encouraged him to dream for better things and go after them. She was his supporter in all things, as he was hers. They worked together for advanced degrees and supported each other no matter what. When she wanted something, he made sure she received it, whether it was a new dress or a new car. They were each together for the long haul. When they took their vows, they really meant "for better or for worse."

My sister and I were blessed far beyond what we deserve with these two as our parents. Kim and I are both adopted, from different states, nine years apart. Faced with years of infertility, my parents acted on their desire to have children by applying to adopt an infant. After completing the numerous steps involved in adoption, like credit reports, home studies, and intensive/invasive interviews, my parents were approved to adopt. A while later, my parents were selected as, well, my parents. The couple was turning into a family.

After years of being childless, a baby girl was joining the family and things would never be the same. Just nine short years later, after their first baby girl had initiated them into parenthood, a second baby girl staked her claim on all their hearts. The girls shared some sibling rivalry, but being so many years apart in age, the normal sibling conventions were displaced. Instead of an intense rivalry, the sisters shared a devotion rarely found in two females bound by kinship, not by blood.

We had a typical childhood, filled with trampolines, ponies, and athletic events. We played softball, rode bicycles, and had sleepovers. We each received a car to drive when we turned sixteen. We were active in school clubs and athletics and neither my sister nor I had trouble any making friends. My parents always opened their home to all of our friends, and we both have great memories of gatherings at their house. We had birthday parties and Thanksgiving gatherings. We had movie nights with popcorn and friends. Our yard was rolled with toilet paper as a prank in the fall and we decorated the outside of the house with Christmas lights in the winter. We shot fireworks on the Fourth of July and gave away Halloween candy to the few trick or treating kids in the neighborhood. We played Kick the Can with the neighbor kids and built clubhouses. We roller-skated on our cul de sac, buried our dead pets in the backyard, and picked figs, strawberries, and tomatoes from the garden.

My sister and I, while as different as night and day, have a bond that cannot be broken, regardless of the circumstances. Do we disagree? Certainly. Do we get on each other's nerves? Of course. Will we forever support the other, including at times of heartbreak and despair? Without a doubt. We may face troubling times, but we will face them together. Our faith in humanity may be shaken, but our resolve is strong. At the end of the day, there is nothing we cannot face together. My parents were not rich, but my sister and I did not go without anything we needed. It is only now, as adults, we can realize the sacrifices our parents made to ensure we had whatever we needed, and many of the things we wanted. They provided us with the emotional and material things that were necessary to be prepared to face adulthood head-on. We made them parents; they made us theirs.

Six Years More

By my nature, I am an eternal optimist. Through my rose-colored glasses, I see the liquid halfway full in the glass. I can usually find a way to put a positive spin on a situation. If it is raining, at least there are no tornados. If the sun is shining brightly, I am glad someone invented sunscreen. I rarely face a time when I cannot find something positive about the situation. My father's death actually has a positive spin as well. Were any of us ready for him to die? Will we ever be the same? Absolutely not. Will I forever consider myself blessed to know him? You had better believe it!

I fully believe God used my father's death to His advantage. Now, months after Dad's death I begin to realize how God actually blessed us all during Pop's illness and death. Years ago, my father was ill, on the verge of death, from two different unusual afflictions. One was Pulmonary Eosinophilia, a condition when the lungs fill with eosinophils, which our bodies produce, but not in the amounts found in his body. We believe this condition was the result of an allergic reaction. Dad was

132

misdiagnosed as having viral pneumonia, and only transferring him to UAB by critical care ambulance brought a clear diagnosis. This illness brought numerous lung washes and biopsies, and a stay of many days in ICU. Eventually he recovered enough to return home, but his immune system was weakened from high doses of steroids. Due to his weakened state, we think he inhaled a fungal spore from hay bales at his farm. A fungus took hold in his lungs and began to grow. Again, he was treated at UAB. He suffered through multiple IV and oral antifungal medications and steroids. Eventually, he was released to return home and continue treatment with home health nurses. My father contracted two illnesses that could have resulted in death. The odds of him surviving one of these diseases are outrageous. Imagine the odds of surviving both. Incredible. The fact that my father lived another six years shows the mercy and grace of the Lord. Each additional day with my father was a gift; one not to be taken lightly; one that earned praises from us.

I fully believe God knew my family was not prepared to lose my father from those two illnesses. He would have missed so many things that happened within our family. Six years is a long time. Imagine all the changes that occur within a family over the course of six years. His last granddaughter had not been born. His first granddaughter had not attended a prom or received her driver's license; his second granddaughter had not played soccer or performed in a dance recital. His grandson had not yet played football or basketball. My father had not yet made it to his milestone of fifty years of marriage. He would not have been there when my mom got sick but refused to go to the doctor and he called me to take her. He had not yet been inducted into our county's athletic Hall of Fame. He had not had the opportunity to see his granddaughter receive awards for her volleyball prowess or see her picture in the local newspaper at the county varsity track meet. He had not heard his grandson's name called out for making a tackle or watched him at his induction into the National Junior Beta Club. Dad would have missed the joy of hearing his namesake baby girl call him Poppa. He had not yet

134

watched his second granddaughter perform her part on stage during a school program. He would have missed all the love his grandchildren gave, and they would surely have missed having him around for their milestones. God gave my father and all of us an extra six years together. I think God kept my father alive to see these things—to enjoy the adventures of his grandchildren—to bless us again.

I believe that God waited to take my father home until my mom, my sister, and I were a little more ready. Now, I do not mean that we were really ready. Even knowing the inevitable was fast approaching, I was not ready. I do not know that I could ever have been ready to watch my father pass into his Heavenly reward. However, I am certain that I was not ready, mentally, six years ago. I do not think my sister and my mom were prepared either. I believe God gave us this extra time to prepare. Many of my friends have lost their fathers in the last six years. This experience of watching and grieving with them gave me some newfound empathy about the loss of a parent. I would not have been emotionally stable enough, six years ago, to withstand such a loss. It is difficult now. It would have been impossible for me then. I know that God had a reason.

Perhaps we had not yet met the right people to help us through this crisis. We had plenty of friends, but maybe certain ones have left an impact through words or a kindness that we would not have had earlier. I know I have friendships now that were merely acquaintances a few years back. I do not know that I could have accepted so easily that God was in charge if my father had passed away years ago. Maybe I would have been angrier, bitter, or unable to embrace the new role that I have undertaken in my family. What I do know is that I am willing to accept that God had His hand on my family during all the trials and tribulations of my father's journey from diagnosis to death. Without that comfort, I would not be able to function at a rational level.

Perhaps those people who helped us in so many ways, by lending their homes, providing meals, offering support, might not have been able to do so many years ago. What are the odds that we would be offered housing in exactly the two towns we needed to take my dad for treatment? We received so many whole meals that we never wanted for anything to eat during the entire horrible process. We had so many people praying, so many that I cannot even begin to guess a number, many of whom did not know my father, just knew his story. Maybe God gave us six years to let those who ministered to us have time to get where they needed to be. I know some of my father's former ball players were located in other states. Perhaps they would not have been able to visit or see him if his death had not been just as God had planned it. I do not know why God gave us that extra time, but I am forever grateful that He chose to allow us the moments we all needed with our husband and father.

Double Vision

Hindsight is twenty-twenty. Looking back on this terrible journey with my father, I realize that God arranged for so many things to happen, and so many people to be in the right place at the right time—or at least when we needed them. I have said before that God was not surprised to see my father in Heaven. He was also not surprised by any of the decisions we made, or the possibilities we considered. God had a hand in putting the things and people we needed directly in our path, even before we knew we needed them. Without a doubt, we serve a God that has a plan for each of us. My father's plan was in place long before we knew he was sick. We followed the plan God had for him, and our family, without even knowing we were doing so. Looking back, I can easily see that God had made all the arrangements for us before we knew we would need them. He provided us places to stay, the financial ability to gain at least some peace of mind about the treatment, and comfort and fond memories at the end of it all.

My father was scheduled to begin his chemotherapy at UAB in October. His treatment began with intravenous medicines for nausea and allergic reactions. These pre-medicines took around two hours to administer. After that, he received a combination of four different drugs that comprised the CHOP chemotherapy regimen. One was administered directly from a syringe into his chest port. The other drugs were dripped into the port from IV bags. The entire treatment lasted most all day. At the end of the day, he was tired, but not often nauseated. He needed to return the next day to receive an injection of a medicine to increase his white blood cell growth. Chemotherapy is designed to strip the body of anything in its way. Chemo kills both the good and bad cells, not just the bad or damaged ones. In return, the patient's body is sloughing off all the dying cells, which contain both healthy and cancer cells. The patient then is at a great risk for contracting an infection or additional illness due to the loss of cells that fuel the immune system. This injection was designed to increase the cells that help fight off infection.

Because my family lives over an hour away from UAB, having my father near in case of distress was a worry for us. Mom and Dad could have opted to stay at a local motel, or a nearby lodge for cancer patients. Instead, Robert and Florence Hall, Mom and Dad's friends from college, offered their home in Hoover. They own a duplex and their son and his wife, John and Ana, live in one side along with their young boys. The other side is vacant, but furnished. The ability to stay in this home, with neighbors they knew nearby, was such a blessing to my family. The first time that Mom and Dad stayed at the Hoover house, Kim and I drove with them from UAB to help get them acquainted to the neighborhood and find an easy way back to the hospital if necessary. John and Ana met us at the door. Ana had prepared a meal for my folks, and John helped my dad find the television remote and ESPN. Kim and I drove to a nearby pharmacy to pick up a few things they needed, as well as some cold drinks and snacks. Mom had packed her van with items she thought they might need, but the house was so well stocked, almost nothing she brought was necessary. Kim and I returned home, thankful for all the Halls and the provisions made on my mom and dad's behalf.

Timing is Everything

I did not think about the timing or availability of the Hoover house until recently. Perhaps I should have considered how perfectly that fit into our plans. Kim and I were prepared to spend the night, but that would have necessitated us taking additional days off work. The Lord was watching out for my sister and me just as He had His hand on my parents. That chemo trip was successfully completed and my parents returned home the next day, after the injection. My father had no real side effects from the first chemo infusion. We prayed that the others would be about the same. We were wrong. My father did become increasingly ill as the treatments progressed. At one point, he was so sick, John had to drive Mom and Dad back to UAB. Dad stayed overnight, but the sickness seemed to pass and he was released the next day. This was a time that I was exceedingly overjoyed about Mom having John and Ana as neighbors in the Hoover house. Mom was upset and in no shape to drive. Dad needed Mom's attention because he was so ill. John was the lifesaver, driving them to the hospital and staying with them until it was determined Dad would be admitted. How can I look at these actions and think that God had left us to make do on our own? Now, it is plain to see that God was the driving force behind the Hoover house and the blessings that we received from the family. More than fifty years have passed since my parents met Robert and Florence Hall. God designed that meeting long ago, in order to have them provide for my parents' needs at this time.

When my father was diagnosed with a second type of lymphoma, we decided to seek another opinion at M.D. Anderson Cancer Center in Houston, Texas. Financially, my parents could afford the trip and would be able to stay for an extended time, if necessary, at local hospital lodging. This was not how they had envisioned spending their retirement funds, but desperate times call for desperate measures. The waiting list for lodging through the hospital was long, and we were still undetermined about the length of stay, or if we would all return to UAB for additional treatment. We opted to stay at a local hotel, pending the initial visit with an oncologist. We hoped to have some idea of necessary length of treatment, as well as if we should return home or remain in Texas for the treatment. Here began another blessing.

When my uncle found out we were going to Houston, he told my mom that one of their relatives had a daughter who lived there. We were leery of calling a relative we did not know to ask if we could all invade her home, so my uncle handled that for us. A phone call later, and that relative, sweet Peggy Born, had opened her home to us for an indefinite stay. I was so worried that we would impede Peggy's routine. I mean, there were three of us driving in to stay, and then my sister flew in as well. Peggy's party of one had just gained four new members. You cannot imagine how pleased we were to have a home, just twenty minutes away from MDA, to stay at during the trip. Just think, to have laundry facilities, a full kitchen, a Keurig coffeemaker, and comfortable beds—these small things made us so happy. I know I would have been fine in a hotel, but the luxury of living in a house was undeniable. We were all overjoyed.

Peggy was so good to us the entire time. She gave us keys to her house, told us the best grocery stores, and advised us on good places to eat and shop. She cooked for us, washed clothes for us, and cared for us. When my father was in the hospital, my sister and I still stayed at Peggy's home. Mom stayed with my dad at the hospital and only occasionally left. Peggy dropped in with milkshakes and treats for both my parents. She sent leftovers so Mom could have something besides the hospital fast food. I cannot imagine the differences we would have experiences without Peggy there to help us. She even added ESPN to her cable package so Dad would be able to watch his favorite sports. Peggy went out of her way, physically and financially, to provide for my family. I only hope that one day I can pay forward the generosity that we have received. I know God placed Peggy and her sweet spirit in Houston to provide for us. She was truly placed by God to help us in our time of need.

Sweet Summertime Blues

The blessing my sister and I received after the Houston trip was one that only school teachers will understand. My father first began this horrendous journey in September of 2012. My sister and I had been at school for only a few weeks in the year when we got the terrible news. The Lord provided my father with time to live throughout the school year. Most of his trouble came in June. We were both out of school for the summer and able to travel and just spend time with Dad. The summer was the best and worst of our lives. My sister and I were able to stay with my folks, almost every day during the summer. Oh, we had a few things to do, some workshops to attend, a few summer athletic events to coach, but overall, we could stay at their house and visit with my dad. The grandchildren were out of school and each day, as much as possible, they visited and loved on their Poppa. While we were discouraged that Pop was home with hospice, how could we complain about having this time with him? He had so many visitors, former students and ball players, church members, colleagues from his forty-year career. He welcomed each one and we were there to meet and greet as well. We have pictures of Dad with all his guests. If he knew they were saying goodbye, he never let on about it. He insisted on walking them to their cars and told them all he was proud of the person he or she had become. I know it was difficult for him, but he handled every visit and visitor with grace, but I realized quickly how loved he was by the number of visitors and phone calls he received each day.

As the days of his life drew to a close, my family gathered around the man who had meant so much to all of us. We laughed about his pranks and antics. We prayed for his suffering to end, and his death to happen peacefully. We continued our limited, mundane lives. Visitors were turned away. Family members were called and placed on alert. We stayed at the house, with no other recourse, waiting for him to die.

Many events have happened since my father's death. Most of them are simply troubles that come from living on Earth and dealing with other people. I have heard other people say they have had signs that let them know everything was perfectly fine with their lost loved one. I have not always believed that, but I accepted that some comfort was derived from the supposed sign. Now, I understand that completely.

My father was a teacher and coach at a college that has a cardinal as a mascot. My nieces call it "the big red bird." This spring, as winter is finally fading, I have taken the opportunity to enjoy a morning cup of coffee on my porch. This is where I spend my quiet time—time before the kids awake and the day gets too busy for prayer and reflection. I enjoy the solitude of the chilly mornings, watching the sky to see the beautiful sunlight piercing the clouds, and thank God for another day on Earth. I look at the yard, admiring the beauty of the trees and bushes that are beginning their new growth. How blessed I am, each morning, to enjoy all the Lord has given me, just in my backyard.

Every day for the past couple of weeks, a cardinal has visited the back yard, playing with other birds, but staying well away from the cat. I have never noticed the cardinal in my yard before. Perhaps I have not chosen to slow down and look at all the creations in the yard. Maybe the cardinal appeared here this year, just for me. I believe this is another God moment for me. I think it is simply His way of telling me to be faithful, to know my father is fine, to know we will all recover, eventually. All I really know is, seeing that red bird gives me some semblance of peace.

Just next month, my mom, sister, and I will award the Riley Whitaker Memorial Scholarship to one deserving student headed to Gadsden State Community College next fall. I am certain that day will be extremely difficult for all of us. While I know my father would be happy to play a part in sending a young adult to college, the rest of us realize that there would be no need for the scholarship if he were still alive. It is, indeed, a mixed blessing. How he would love it; yet, how sad we are.

My dad was the epitome of a family man. He loved us all with all that he had. He never failed to protect us, until he could protect us no more from the horror that became his death. Our wishes regarding his sickness and death went unheeded, but his acceptance into his Heavenly home more than makes up for the terrible suffering he endured here on Earth. In the end, all I can do is accept my father's death and move on. I will never fully recover from the tragedy my family has faced, but I can live my life to the fullest. My memories will help me travel the path I now follow, the path that has brought me on a closer walk with God. The helpless feeling will fade, as the power of the Heavens brightens my path. I continue to pray for sunshine in my life. I continue to pray for strength to face the upheaval my father's death has caused. I pray for all those who were touched in any way by my father's death. But mostly, I pray for peace.

In-Law Illness

My in-laws are both in bad health. My husband and his brother are dealing with their ailing parents. My father-in-law has Parkinson's Disease, and my mother-in-law suffers from dementia and congestive heart failure. Until recently, their health had been manageable. They had employed a sitter, the same one my family used, to stay overnight as a cautionary measure. Big Ed makes sure baths are done and breakfast is cooked before he leaves in the mornings. Now, my mother in law is in a nursing home waiting for a fractured arm to heal before she can attend a rehabilitation facility to help with her balance. None of this time is easy for my husband and his brother. My husband was by my side throughout my father's illness and death. It is now my turn to hold his hand through his time of trouble. My heart aches for him. I know exactly how he feels. He is exhausted from the physical demands placed on him and his brother. Someone must check on their mom, who is at one place, and then check on their dad, who is at home. I do as much as I can to ease his burdens, but he feels the same responsibility to his parents as I feel/felt toward mine.

He feels helpless. I know he would trade places with either of his parents in a heartbeat if that were possible. He wants to be with them, every minute, for any minute could be their last here on earth. He can do nothing more to help. He and his brother worry. They try to figure out the best way to have some peace about the situation. I have tried to make him understand that no matter what he does, he will never feel that he did enough. He will second-guess every decision. He will play the "What if..." game. He and his brother will often wonder if they should have taken off work and stayed with their folks, if they should have refused to go home for a rest, if they should have insisted that certain procedures be completed, or refused other procedures. Simply put, there is no way that the boys can alter the course set out by God, but we all want to believe that there is something we can do to extend life. Nothing they do or say will, really, make a difference. It may give them both some peace in their hearts that they did the right thing, but, truly, I do not believe anything will change the course already put into action.

In these moments of confusion and worry, I pray for peace for my husband, his brother, and the grandchildren. I pray for my children, especially, as they are still reeling from the loss of my father. I pray that the suffering be limited and the sickness be short, but in the end, the path we follow is already determined. At the end of the day, we must trust in the Lord and His will.

Platitudes of Gratitude

Certain folks have helped me tremendously along the way to writing these stories. Thank you!

Amy, Kathy, and Laurel—you were the best beta test reading posse ever.

Shelly and Kim--you picked me up when I was down. Your words of wisdom gave me comfort.

Jeff—Love you always. Need I say more?

Brennan and Brandt—I love you with all that I am. Read these books when you are ready.

Mom—I am forever here for you. Love you.

Kim—I will always have your back. No matter what. Love you.

Ellie and Riley—D.D loves you. Forever.

Also Available as ebooks by B. Taylor Mason

<u>How I Grieve Series</u>

I Grieve: Praying for Sunshine

I Still Grieve: Praying for Strength

Forever I Grieve: Praying for Peace

11761240R00101

Made in the USA
San Bernardino, CA
28 May 2014